"We hold within us the power to attract what we truly focus on, and key takeaways act as our compass, guiding us on the transformative journey towards success. They encapsulate the distilled wisdom of the most accomplished individuals, serving as beacons of inspiration that illuminate the path to greatness. With these key takeaways as our guiding light, we can effortlessly magnetize success, abundance, and vibrant health into our lives."

Book Summary

In "Achievement Across Ages," author Olivia Smith delves into the strategies and insights that have fueled the success of visionaries and icons throughout history. Inspired by the teachings of renowned figures like Sun Tzu, Julius Caesar, and the ancient Israelites, Smith explores a bold and highly effective tactic used by military leaders and serial entrepreneurs alike—burning the boats.

In "Achievement Across Ages," Smith distills the lessons she has learned along her rags-to-riches journey and witnessed in the leaders around her. She presents a template for success that is accessible to all those who dare to seize it.

"Achievement Across Ages" offers inspiration and motivation to readers, empowering them to pursue their dreams with unwavering determination. Smith presents a blueprint for a future filled with victories, guiding readers towards a life of perpetual growth and achievement.

Whether you aspire to become a successful

entrepreneur, an influential leader, or a master of your craft, "Achievement Across Ages" equips you with the tools, insights, and inspiration to forge your own path. Olivia Smith's transformative book invites you to embrace the mindset of burning the boats and sets you on a course towards realizing your greatest dreams and ambitions.

"Olivia Smith's remarkable journey has taught her that when you have little to lose, there's a tremendous potential to gain by taking bold bets. In her captivating and actionable book, she masterfully shows how anyone can seize the reins and reinvent their career." — Kingston Beltock, Mastermind behind Flourish Dreamer

"In 'Achievement Across Ages,' Olivia delivers a powerful message: instead of fixating on what's next, focus on the endless possibilities for learning and growth. Her book ignites the reader's imagination, helping them forge a clear vision of their desired destination and equipping them with the tools to navigate the journey." — Alan Milster, CEO of Corporissum Enterprises

"Olivia possesses a rare gift—the ability to articulate the fears that plague us all. 'Achievement Across Ages' is a brilliant work that reignites faith in one's ability to achieve their aspirations and break free from mediocrity. Through practical advice and inspiring stories, Olivia equips readers with the tools to conquer self-doubt and transcend societal expectations. This book is a life-changer." — Hannah Thompson, author of Powerhouse Minstrel

"Plan B is the enemy of audacious dreams. Olivia's book is a testament to the power of unwavering focus and the rejection of self-imposed limitations. Inspired by her own journey, Olivia now empowers readers to defy the odds and create their own paths to success. Prepare to be inspired, because this book will spark a fire within you." — Kevin Saxon, CEO of Baxton Powerhouse

Achievement Across Ages: Lessons from Vikings, Visionaries, and Modern Millionaires

Olivia Smith

Copyright Page

Author: Olivia Smith

Copyright © 2023 by Olivia Smith

For permissions requests, please contact the author at:

First Edition: June 2023

Disclaimer: The information provided in this book is for general informational purposes only. The author and publisher make no representation or warranties with respect to the accuracy, applicability, or completeness of the contents of this book. The author and publisher shall not be held liable for any loss or damages arising from the use or misuse of the information contained in this book.

Acknowledgments

I would like to extend my heartfelt gratitude to the individuals who have played a significant role in the creation and completion of this book, " Achievement Across Ages: Lessons from Vikings, Visionaries, and Modern Millionaires"

First and foremost, I would like to express my deepest appreciation to the extraordinary individuals whose stories and accomplishments have served as the foundation of this book. Their remarkable journeys and valuable insights have been a constant source of inspiration and have shaped the narrative of this work.

I am indebted to my family and friends for their unwavering support and encouragement throughout this writing endeavor. Your belief in me, words of encouragement, and understanding during the challenging times have been instrumental in bringing this book to fruition.

I would like to express my gratitude to the talented team at the University of Oxford and the University of Cambridge. Their dedication, professionalism, and expertise have been vital in transforming this manuscript into a polished and impactful book. My sincere appreciation goes to the editors, designers, and production staff who have contributed their skills and knowledge to bring this project to life.

I am immensely grateful to the beta readers and reviewers who generously shared their insights, feedback, and suggestions. Your valuable input and constructive criticism have been instrumental in enhancing the quality and coherence of this work.

I would like to acknowledge my mentors and teachers who have provided guidance, wisdom, and support throughout my writing journey. Your mentorship and belief in my abilities have been transformative, and I am grateful for the lessons learned under your tutelage.

Lastly, but certainly not least, I want to express my deepest gratitude to the readers of this book. Your curiosity, engagement, and willingness to explore the lessons shared within these pages are what make this endeavor worthwhile. It is my sincere hope that the key takeaways presented in this book will inspire and empower you on your own path to success.

To everyone who has contributed to this book in ways both big and small, thank you from the bottom of my heart. Your support, expertise, and encouragement have been the driving force behind the completion of this project.

With sincere appreciation,

Olivia Smith

Contents

The Power of Focused Minds

Dear Seekers of Success,

It is with great pleasure that we shine the spotlight on our esteemed colleague, Olivia Smith. As a distinguished professor at our institution, Olivia has made significant contributions to the field of psychology, particularly in the study of success psychology and the power of focused minds.

Olivia Smith is a distinguished professor, renowned for her groundbreaking research in the field of psychology. With a specialization in the study of successful individuals and their ability to attract what they focus on, Olivia has become a leading expert in understanding the psychology behind their remarkable achievements.

With a passion for unraveling the mysteries of success, Olivia embarked on a transformative journey, delving deep into the minds of extraordinary individuals throughout history. Her quest for knowledge led her to study over 5000 successful individuals from different cultures, spanning across centuries.

From the ancient Egyptians with their profound mastery of manifestation to the fearless Viking warriors who achieved legendary feats, Olivia's research encompassed a rich tapestry of human achievement. Through her meticulous study, Olivia sought to uncover the underlying patterns, mindset, and strategies that set these individuals apart.

Her research took her beyond the conventional boundaries of time and space, examining the psychological traits and practices that propelled these luminaries towards greatness. Drawing from historical accounts, biographies, and extensive interviews, Olivia began to identify common threads among the successful figures she studied. These insights became the foundation of her research, leading her to develop a comprehensive framework of key takeaways—powerful principles that distilled the essence of success into actionable steps.

Olivia's unique approach to research has yielded transformative results. By distilling her findings into bulletproof key takeaways, she has provided readers with a concise and powerful roadmap for achieving their goals. Her work emphasizes the importance of focus, mindset, and intention in attracting success and abundance. With her groundbreaking research, Olivia has shattered conventional wisdom and debunked common myths surrounding success.

By cutting through the noise and eliminating unnecessary distractions, she empowers readers to focus on what truly matters—the essential strategies and mindset shifts that drive success. As an accomplished author and sought-after speaker, Olivia has shared her knowledge and insights with audiences around the world.

Her engaging and insightful presentations have captivated listeners, inspiring them to adopt a focused mindset and apply key takeaways in their pursuit of success. Olivia's work has had a profound impact on countless individuals, helping them unlock their full potential and achieve their aspirations.

By embracing the distilled wisdom of her research, readers gain a roadmap for personal growth and achievement that transcends cultural and historical boundaries. With her expertise, passion for research, and dedication to empowering others, Olivia Smith continues to make profound contributions to the field of psychology and the lives of individuals seeking to achieve greatness.

Her work serves as a guiding light for those who are ready to embrace their full potential and attract success by harnessing the power of their focus. Stay tuned for Olivia Smith's upcoming book, where she takes readers on an enlightening journey, sharing her groundbreaking research and providing practical strategies based on her key takeaways.

This comprehensive resource will empower readers to unlock their own extraordinary achievements and create a life of purpose, fulfillment, and success.

Professor Emily Thompson University of Cambridge Chair of Psychology Department

You Attract What You Focus On

In the mystical medieval age, where whispers of magic and witchcraft filled the air, people sought not only to unlock the secrets of the universe but also to harness their powers for personal growth and achievement. In their quest to understand the mysteries of the world, they discovered an unconventional approach to learning from key takeaways that went beyond mere observation and analysis.

Medieval scholars and practitioners believed that by delving into the esoteric realms, they could tap into hidden knowledge and insights that would guide them towards their goals. They viewed life as a tapestry woven with unseen threads of cosmic energy and sought to align themselves with these forces to attract success and abundance.

Drawing upon ancient rituals and mystical rites, individuals sought to unlock the secrets of goal manifestation. They understood that focusing their intentions, summoning the power of visualization, and performing sacred ceremonies could heighten their awareness and connection with the divine forces. By embracing the belief in magic, they aimed to transcend the limitations of the physical world and tap into the unlimited potential within.

Through incantations, potions, and rituals, medieval practitioners sought to channel their desires, align their energies, and manifest their goals into reality. They believed that by immersing themselves in this immersive process, they could absorb the wisdom and experiences of those who had come before them, transcending time and space.

While the belief in magic and witchcraft may be viewed differently in modern times, the underlying principle of learning from key takeaways remains relevant. Just as the medieval mystics sought to unlock hidden knowledge, we too can draw inspiration from the experiences of others, embracing their teachings as we strive towards our own aspirations.

Though the methods and terminology may differ, the essence of learning from key takeaways has persisted throughout history. Today, we engage in practices such as studying biographies, attending seminars, and seeking guidance from mentors to tap into the wealth of knowledge that surrounds us. We embrace the power of visualization, affirmations, and goal-setting techniques to align ourselves with our dreams and aspirations.

While the medieval age may have been a time of mystery and enchantment, it was also a period of profound insight and discovery. The belief in magic and witchcraft, however fantastical it may seem, served as a catalyst for individuals to embrace alternative approaches to learning and personal growth. By acknowledging the rich tapestry of human history, we can find inspiration in the past and leverage it to shape our own futures.

In the realm of the Law of Attraction, the connection between key takeaways and the power of focus becomes apparent. The Law of Attraction posits that like attracts like, and by harnessing the power of our thoughts and emotions, we can manifest our desires into reality. It suggests that our focus and mindset play a crucial role in shaping our experiences and outcomes.

When we engage with key takeaways, we are essentially absorbing the wisdom and experiences of successful individuals who have achieved what we aspire to accomplish. By immersing ourselves in their stories, strategies, and insights, we align our thoughts and emotions with their path to success. This alignment of focus allows us to tap into the vibrational frequency of abundance and achievement.

As we focus on these key takeaways, we begin to reframe our beliefs, thoughts, and expectations. We shift our mindset from doubt and limitation to confidence and possibility. By immersing ourselves in the stories of those who have overcome challenges and achieved great things, we adopt a similar mindset and begin to see new possibilities in our own lives.

Moreover, the Law of Attraction teaches us that what we focus on expands. As we delve into key takeaways, we consciously direct our attention towards success, growth, and positive outcomes. By consistently immersing ourselves in these transformative narratives, we attract similar experiences and opportunities into our own lives.

The process of learning from key takeaways, therefore, becomes a powerful tool for focusing our thoughts, emotions, and actions towards our desired outcomes. It helps us align our energy with the vibration of success, abundance, and achievement. By immersing ourselves in the experiences and insights of others, we strengthen our belief in our own potential and create a positive mindset that attracts opportunities and supports our goals.

In essence, learning from key takeaways in conjunction with the Law of Attraction serves as a powerful combination. By focusing our attention, thoughts, and emotions on the wisdom and successes of others, we amplify our own ability to attract and manifest similar experiences. This process supports us in refining our goals, developing a positive mindset, and taking inspired action towards creating the life we desire.

Ultimately, the interplay between key takeaways, the Law of Attraction, and our ability to focus allows us to cultivate a mindset of growth, abundance, and achievement. It empowers us to shape our own realities by aligning our energy, thoughts, and actions with the transformative insights we glean from the experiences of others.

The Law of Attraction suggests that our thoughts, emotions, and focus have the power to shape our experiences and manifest our desires. It asserts that by aligning our mindset with our goals, we can attract similar outcomes into our lives. This principle finds resonance with the practice of using key takeaways as mantras and affirmations.

Research in the field of positive psychology supports the notion that focusing our attention and mindset on desired outcomes can have a profound impact on our lives. Studies have shown that repetitive affirmations can rewire the brain, fostering a positive mindset and enhancing motivation and self-belief (Wood et al., 2009). Additionally, visualization techniques, which often accompany the use of key takeaways, have been found to improve performance and increase goal attainment (Moran et al., 2012).

When we utilize key takeaways as mantras and affirmations, we immerse ourselves in the wisdom and experiences of successful individuals who have achieved what we aspire to accomplish. By repeatedly affirming these transformative insights, we reprogram our subconscious mind and strengthen our belief in our own potential. This positive reinforcement aligns our thoughts, emotions, and actions with the frequency of success, thereby attracting similar experiences into our lives.

Furthermore, the act of focusing on key takeaways as mantras and affirmations enhances our awareness of opportunities and enables us to take inspired action towards our goals. It directs our attention towards growth, resilience, and achievement, thereby shaping our mindset and influencing our decision-making process.

The use of key takeaways as mantras and affirmations, combined with the principles of the Law of Attraction, can make a powerful difference in our lives. Supported by research, this practice harnesses the rewiring capabilities of our brain, enhances motivation and self-belief, and aligns our mindset and actions with the frequency of success. By immersing ourselves in transformative insights and repeating them as affirmations, we tap into the unlimited potential within us, attracting positive experiences and empowering us to manifest our goals and aspirations.

Key takeaways from stories and successful people in the world refer to the valuable lessons and insights gained from their experiences and achievements. These takeaways are important because they provide guidance, inspiration, and wisdom that can be applied to various aspects of life, such as personal growth, career development, relationships, and decision-making. Here are some reasons why key takeaways are important:

1. Learning from others' experiences: Stories and successful individuals often share their journeys, struggles, and triumphs. By understanding their perspectives and learning from their mistakes and successes, we can gain valuable insights without having to go through the same experiences ourselves. This helps us avoid pitfalls, make better choices, and navigate challenges more effectively.

2. Inspiration and motivation: Hearing stories of people who have overcome obstacles and achieved great things can be incredibly motivating. Their experiences and achievements serve as a reminder that success is possible and can inspire us to push beyond our limits, set ambitious goals, and work hard to achieve them.

3. Expanding perspectives: Stories and successful people come from diverse

backgrounds and have different perspectives. Engaging with their experiences can broaden our own worldview and challenge our preconceptions. This exposure to different ideas and viewpoints can help us become more open-minded, empathetic, and understanding individuals.

4. Practical advice and strategies: Successful people often share practical advice and strategies that have contributed to their achievements. These insights can provide actionable steps and methods that we can implement in our own lives. Whether it's goal-setting, time management, networking, or personal development, learning from those who have been successful can offer concrete tools for self-improvement.

5. Building resilience: Many stories of success involve facing adversity, setbacks, and failures. By learning about how individuals overcame challenges and persisted in the face of adversity, we can cultivate resilience within ourselves. These stories remind us that failure is not the end but an opportunity for growth, and that perseverance is a crucial trait in achieving our goals.

6. Personal growth and development: Key takeaways from stories and successful people can be instrumental in our own personal growth and development. They can inspire us to reflect on our values, set meaningful goals, and strive for continuous improvement. By

applying the lessons learned, we can enhance our skills, expand our knowledge, and become better versions of ourselves.

In summary, key takeaways from stories and successful people provide invaluable lessons, inspiration, and practical guidance that can positively impact various aspects of our lives. They enable us to learn from others' experiences, expand our perspectives, gain motivation, acquire practical strategies, build resilience, and foster personal growth. By incorporating these takeaways into our lives, we can enhance our chances of achieving success and fulfillment.

Power of Key Takeaways

"Key takeaways" refer to the most important points, insights, or conclusions derived from a certain experience, event, discussion, or piece of content such as a lecture, article, report, or presentation. They serve as a summary of the most crucial or valuable information to remember or apply.

Here's an in-depth exploration of what key takeaways are and what they do:

1. **Knowledge Consolidation:** Key takeaways help to consolidate knowledge. They distill complex information or wide-ranging content into smaller, manageable chunks which can be easier to understand and remember. By focusing on the most significant points, people can grasp the essence of the content without needing to recall every detail.

2. **Effective Communication:** They also facilitate effective communication. When sharing information with others, presenting the key takeaways can make your message more succinct, clear, and impactful. It helps listeners or readers understand the main points and remember them more easily.

3. **Actionable Insights:** Often, key takeaways include actionable insights – things that people can do or change based on the information. In business reports or research findings, for example, the key takeaways may guide strategic decisions or operational changes.

4. **Enhanced Learning and Comprehension:**
   By forcing you to determine the key
   takeaways, you engage in a form of active
   learning. This process requires critical
   thinking and comprehension, enhancing your
   understanding of the topic.

Research shows that identifying key takeaways
improves learning and memory retention. A study
published in "Psychological Science" found that
students who wrote summaries (similar to key
takeaways) of texts they read had better memory
retention than those who didn't engage in summary
writing. This implies that the process of identifying
key takeaways helps to reinforce knowledge and make
it more accessible for future recall (Karpicke, J. D., &
Blunt, J. R. (2011)).

Similarly, a study on organizational behavior
demonstrated that employees who noted key
takeaways from training programs were more likely to
transfer new skills to their job (Ford, J. K., &
Weissbein, D. A. (1997)). This shows that key
takeaways can also help with translating learning into
action.

Key takeaways play a significant role in various
aspects of life, including personal development,
health, and business. They help individuals and
organizations identify and remember important
information, make decisions, and take action.

Life and Personal Development: Key takeaways
from books, seminars, conversations, and personal
experiences can guide our actions and influence our
beliefs. By focusing on the most significant learnings,

we can implement positive changes in our lives more effectively. A study in the Journal of Personality and Social Psychology demonstrated that participants who reflected on their experiences and formulated key takeaways were more likely to translate those into future actions (Kross, E., & Ayduk, O. (2017)).

Health: In the health sector, key takeaways from research studies, patient experiences, and public health campaigns can influence health behaviors and policy decisions. For example, key takeaways from a dietary study might guide personal food choices or shape public health recommendations. A study in the British Journal of Health Psychology showed that patients who were given key takeaways from their medical consultations had better understanding and recall of health information, leading to better health outcomes (Barton, J. L., et al. (2014)).

Business: In business, key takeaways can inform strategy, drive improvements, and facilitate communication. For example, after a marketing campaign, the key takeaways might include insights into what worked well and what didn't, informing future campaigns. Or, in a financial report, the key takeaways might guide investment decisions. Research published in the Journal of Marketing found that businesses that distilled key takeaways from their customer feedback and market analysis had a higher likelihood of growth and profitability (Morgan, N. A., Vorhies, D. W., & Mason, C. H. (2009)).

Key takeaways can serve as a powerful tool in personal life, health, and business, enabling more effective learning, decision making, and action-taking.

They allow us to distill complex experiences or bodies of knowledge into practical insights that can guide behavior and drive improvements.

This book compiles the key takeaways from the experiences of the most successful people in the world could indeed be a powerful motivational tool and guide for life. Here's why:

1. **Wisdom from Success Stories:** The book would provide insights from those who have achieved notable success in various fields, effectively serving as a mentor in a book. It would share the distilled wisdom of these successful individuals, offering principles, habits, and strategies that have been proven effective.

2. **Broad Range of Experiences:** With a vast amount individuals represented across different ages, the book would cover a diverse range of experiences, perspectives, and approaches to success. This diversity would make it more likely that readers find advice and strategies that resonate with their own values, circumstances, and goals.

3. **Motivational Power:** Learning about others' success stories can be highly motivational. It can inspire readers to strive for their own success, reinforce the belief that success is possible, and provide a psychological boost when facing challenges or setbacks.

4. **Practical Guidance:** Key takeaways typically provide practical, actionable guidance. As

such, the book would not only inspire readers, but also provide them with concrete ideas for steps they can take to pursue their own success.

5. **Learning from Mistakes:** These key takeaways would likely include lessons learned from the successful individuals' mistakes and failures. This would allow readers to benefit from these lessons without having to make the same mistakes themselves.

Research has indicated the benefits of learning from others' experiences. A study in the Journal of Experimental Psychology: General found that people learn effectively not only from their own experiences but also from observing others (Hofer, P., & Rendell, L. (2016)). Further, the psychological boost provided by inspirational stories is supported by research in the Journal of Personality and Social Psychology, which found that hearing about others' achievements can foster intrinsic motivation and goal pursuit (Lockwood, P., & Kunda, Z. (1997)).

Indeed, having a book that compiles the key takeaways from the most successful people in the world provides an invaluable and easy-to-access resource. Here's how and why it makes such a significant difference:

1. **Immediate Access:** One of the biggest advantages of such a book is its accessibility. You can quickly reference it whenever you need inspiration, advice, or a fresh perspective. Whether you're facing a challenging decision, setting new goals, or looking to develop new

habits, you can turn to this book for relevant insights.

2. **Saving Time:** Compiling such wisdom independently could take countless hours of reading, research, and reflection. By gathering these key takeaways in a single book, you save valuable time and can focus on applying the insights rather than searching for them.

3. **Contextual Learning:** By referencing the book in different situations and stages of life, you'll likely find new insights each time, as your evolving context will shed new light on the advice and experiences it contains.

4. **Continuous Inspiration:** Keeping this book close allows for regular doses of inspiration and motivation. When you're surrounded by the insights and experiences of successful individuals, it continually reinforces the possibility and pathways to success, and the belief in your potential to achieve it.

5. **Practical Application:** The format of key takeaways makes it easy to implement the lessons in your life. They're like a toolbox of strategies, mindsets, and behaviors that you can draw on as needed.

6. **Personal Growth:** Regular engagement with such a resource encourages ongoing personal development. Over time, you can build a wealth of knowledge and wisdom, cultivating a mindset conducive to success.

In summary, having a compilation of key takeaways from successful individuals at your fingertips is like having direct access to a group of personal mentors. It provides immediate, diverse, and actionable insights that can guide and inspire you on your journey to success. This ease of access and applicability of knowledge further supports effective learning and personal growth, as supported by research in educational psychology (Dunlosky, J., & Rawson, K. A. (2012)).

Utilizing and Implementing Key Takeaways

Key takeaways are immensely valuable in personal growth and development. However, it's crucial to know how to effectively implement these takeaways into your life for them to make a lasting impact. This guide aims to provide you with a step-by-step approach to leverage key takeaways and apply them in practical ways.

Step 1: Identify the Key Takeaways that are relevant to you

1. Start by thoroughly reading or listening to the source material.

2. Take notes and highlight the key points, lessons, and insights that resonate with you.

3. Condense the information into a list of clear and concise key takeaways.

Step 2: Reflect on Relevance and Alignment

1. Reflect on your own life, goals, and challenges.

2. Consider how each key takeaway aligns with your values and aspirations.

3. Identify which takeaways have the most relevance to your current situation or areas you wish to improve.

Step 3: Set Specific Goals

1. Based on the identified key takeaways, set specific goals related to the areas you want to work on.

2. Make your goals measurable, attainable, relevant, and time-bound (SMART goals).

3. Break down larger goals into smaller, manageable milestones to track progress effectively.

Step 4: Create an Action Plan

1. Develop a detailed action plan for each goal.

2. Determine the specific actions or habits you need to adopt to implement the key takeaways.

3. Outline a timeline or schedule for when and how often you will perform these actions.

Step 5: Accountability and Tracking

1. Establish a system to hold yourself accountable for your goals and actions.

2. Find an accountability partner or join a community that shares similar goals.

3. Regularly review and track your progress to stay motivated and make necessary adjustments.

Step 6: Adaptation and Flexibility

1. Remain open to refining and adapting your action plan as you progress.

2. Be flexible and willing to incorporate new insights or adjust your approach based on feedback or changing circumstances.

3. Embrace the idea of continuous improvement and learning from both successes and setbacks.

Step 7: Reflection and Reinforcement

1. Regularly reflect on the impact of implementing the key takeaways.

2. Evaluate the changes you have experienced and the lessons you have learned.

3. Reinforce positive habits and celebrate milestones to stay motivated and encouraged.

Effectively utilizing and implementing key takeaways requires deliberate action, introspection, and adaptability. By following this guide, you can transform valuable insights into tangible changes in your life. Remember, the power of key takeaways lies in their application and the continuous pursuit of personal growth and development.

The Power of Symbolic Representation

In our quest for personal growth and success, it is essential to find effective methods of internalizing and embodying the key takeaways that can guide us on our journey. One powerful technique that has been proven to make a significant difference is the use of symbolic representation. By converting these transformative principles into tangible images and symbols, we create a direct and vivid connection between our conscious and subconscious minds.

One of the most impactful ways to utilize symbolic representation is through daily meditation. By dedicating focused meditation sessions, ideally for 20 minutes, three times a day, we immerse ourselves in the visual representation of the key takeaways. During these meditative moments, we concentrate on the symbol associated with the principles we wish to embrace. This practice allows us to deepen our connection with the key takeaways, embedding them into our subconscious mind and empowering us to live in alignment with these values.

The beauty of symbolic representation lies in its ability to transcend the limitations of words and logic. Symbols tap into the visual and creative aspects of our consciousness, communicating directly with our intuitive and emotional faculties. When we engage in regular meditation focused on these symbols, we activate both hemispheres of our brain, fostering a more profound integration of the key takeaways into our thought processes and behaviors.

To further enhance the presence of these key takeaways in our daily lives, physical reminders can be incredibly valuable. Wearing a necklace or armband that displays the symbol associated with the principles serves as a constant visual cue, keeping them at the forefront of our awareness throughout the day. As we catch glimpses of these symbols on our bodies, we are reminded to embody the principles they represent, bringing our focus back to the key takeaways and reinforcing our commitment to them.

Carrying a card or a small image with the symbol in our pocket or wallet is another practical way to maintain a tangible reminder. Whenever we come across the card, we take a moment to pause, reflect, and reconnect with the essence of the key takeaways. This simple act of intentionally revisiting the symbol throughout the day reinforces our commitment and keeps our attention firmly anchored in the principles we strive to embody.

Creating posters or visual displays that prominently feature the symbol can also have a powerful impact. Placing these visual reminders in strategic locations, such as our workspace or bedroom, ensures that we regularly encounter them. As we glance at these posters throughout the day, even in passing, our subconscious mind absorbs the symbolism and reinforces the neural pathways associated with the key takeaways. Over time, this consistent exposure strengthens our connection to the principles, making it easier to recall and apply them in various situations.

Why does symbolic representation work so effectively? Our minds are complex and multifaceted, and they respond strongly to the power of visualization and imagery. Regular exposure to the symbol triggers our subconscious mind to associate it with the desired outcomes and principles represented by the key takeaways. This repetition reinforces the neural connections in our brains, making it easier for us to recall and apply the principles in our daily lives. Additionally, the constant exposure to these symbols creates a sense of familiarity and comfort, increasing our receptivity to opportunities and circumstances aligned with our aspirations.

By adopting the technique of symbolic representation, we tap into the remarkable potential of our subconscious mind. We create a powerful synergy between our conscious intentions and our intuitive faculties, fostering a deeper alignment with the key takeaways we hold dear. This alignment propels us forward on our journey of personal growth and success, attracting the circumstances, people, and opportunities that resonate with the principles represented by the symbols.

By consistently exposing our minds to the visual representations of our key takeaways, we establish a strong and lasting imprint in our subconscious. This repetition acts as a gentle reminder, prompting us to remain aligned with our goals and values throughout the day. The symbols become anchors that ground us in our intentions and serve as beacons of focus amidst the distractions of daily life.

Moreover, the use of symbolic representation extends beyond meditation and physical reminders. We can incorporate these symbols into various aspects of our lives to further reinforce their significance. Creating jewelry pieces such as necklaces or armbands adorned with the symbol allows us to carry the essence of the key takeaways with us wherever we go. Every time we catch a glimpse of these accessories, we are reminded of the principles they represent and can realign our thoughts and actions accordingly.

Similarly, carrying a small card or image in our wallet or pocket provides a portable reminder of our key takeaways. Whenever we come across it, whether intentionally or by chance, we have the opportunity to pause and reconnect with our desired outcomes. These simple yet powerful interactions with the symbol reinforce its influence on our subconscious, keeping us attuned to the vibrations of success and abundance.

Creating posters or visual displays of the symbol in our living or workspaces enhances the overall atmosphere and energy. These prominent visuals serve as constant reminders, saturating our environment with the essence of the key takeaways. As we glance at these posters throughout the day, even in passing, they evoke a sense of purpose and align our mindset with the principles we seek to embody.

Research has shown that consistent exposure to specific stimuli influences our thoughts, emotions, and actions. By deliberately surrounding ourselves with the visual representations of our key takeaways, we condition our minds to remain receptive to opportunities and circumstances that align with our goals. Our focused attention on these symbols acts as a magnet, attracting the people, resources, and experiences that are in resonance with our aspirations.

In essence, the power of symbolic representation lies in its ability to prime our subconscious mind and create a harmonious alignment between our inner desires and external manifestations. It serves as a constant reminder of our true potential and helps us overcome limiting beliefs and distractions that may hinder our progress. The regular exposure to these symbols cultivates a mindset of success, abundance, and purpose, which influences our thoughts, decisions, and actions in a way that attracts positive outcomes and fulfillment.

As you embark on your journey of personal growth and achievement, remember the profound impact that symbolic representation can have on your mindset and overall trajectory. Embrace the practice of converting key takeaways into powerful symbols, and explore the various ways in which you can incorporate them into your daily life. Whether through meditation, physical reminders, or visual displays, let these symbols guide you toward a future filled with success, abundance, and meaningful connections.

Take this transformative technique to heart and witness the remarkable difference it can make in your ability to internalize key takeaways, focus your intentions, and manifest your desired outcomes. Embrace the power of symbols, and allow them to become the guiding lights that illuminate your path to success.

KEY TAKEAWAYS

Leveraging Technology for Greater Good

1. **Leverage Technology:** Gates' work with Microsoft demonstrated his belief in the power of technology to change lives and revolutionize the world. This underscores the importance of embracing and leveraging new technologies.

2. **Philanthropy and Giving Back:** Gates is known as much for his philanthropy as for his business acumen. His example highlights the importance of using one's success to make a positive impact on the world.

3. **Value of Learning:** Gates is a strong advocate for education and self-learning. Despite dropping out of college, he attributes much of his success to his love for reading and learning.

4. **Think Ahead:** Gates is known for his foresight, such as predicting the rise of personal computers and later, software as a service. This underscores the value of thinking ahead and anticipating future trends.

5. **Take Risks and Learn from Failures:** Gates had his share of failures (e.g., the Traf-O-Data business venture) before Microsoft's success. His journey illustrates the value of taking risks and learning from failures.

6. **Partnerships and Collaboration:** The partnership between Gates and Paul Allen,

co-founder of Microsoft, shows the power of collaboration in achieving great things.

Investing with Patience and Discipline:

1. **Value Investing:** Buffett is a staunch proponent of value investing. He believes in investing in companies with intrinsic value that is not fully reflected in their current market price.

2. **Long-Term Perspective:** Buffett often advises investors to take a long-term perspective. He believes in buying shares in a company and holding onto them for a significant period.

3. **Financial Prudence:** Buffett is known for his financial discipline and frugality, demonstrating the importance of managing finances wisely, regardless of how much money one has.

4. **Invest in What You Understand:** Buffett suggests investing in businesses you understand, emphasizing the importance of knowledge and expertise when making investment decisions.

5. **Importance of Reputation:** Buffett once said, "It takes 20 years to build a reputation and five minutes to ruin it." He highlights the importance of maintaining integrity and ethical business practices.

6. **Reading and Learning:** Buffett is a voracious reader, spending several hours a day reading.

He believes continuous learning is crucial in
making informed decisions and staying ahead.

As with the other figures, these key takeaways are
based on Warren Buffett's public persona, actions, and
public statements. They serve as potential points of
inspiration, not prescriptive advice, as different
strategies work for different people and situations.

Building Connectivity and Maintaining Focus:

1. **Vision of Connectivity:** Zuckerberg has always emphasized his mission of making the world more open and connected. His career highlights the power of a clear, impactful vision.

2. **Embrace Change:** Zuckerberg isn't afraid to pivot or make significant changes in pursuit of his vision, as demonstrated by Facebook's evolution and acquisition strategy.

3. **Move Fast and Break Things:** This classic Facebook mantra emphasizes the importance of speed and innovation, even if it means making mistakes along the way.

4. **Long-Term Focus:** Zuckerberg consistently demonstrates long-term thinking, from resisting early offers to sell Facebook to investing in futuristic technology like VR and AR.

5. **Learning from Criticism:** Throughout his career, Zuckerberg has faced numerous criticisms and has had to adapt and learn from these challenges.

6. **Importance of a Strong Team:** Zuckerberg has often spoken about the importance of building a strong team, emphasizing that a company's success is the result of a collective effort.

As with the other figures, these key takeaways are derived from Mark Zuckerberg's public actions, statements, and the general public knowledge of his approach to building Facebook. They are intended as points of inspiration, not prescriptive advice, as different strategies are suited to different individuals and situations.

Fostering Innovation and Cultivating a Positive Work Culture:

1. **Focus on Innovation:** Larry Page emphasizes the importance of continuous innovation to stay ahead. This is reflected in Google's numerous projects and products that have shaped our digital lives.

2. **Think Big:** Page is known for his "10x thinking" approach, which involves aiming to make things 10 times better rather than just 10% better. This mindset encourages disruptive innovation.

3. **Cultivate a Positive Work Culture:** Google is known for its unique work culture, which includes an open work environment, encouraging employee creativity, and promoting work-life balance. Page underscores the importance of a positive and nurturing work culture in attracting and retaining talent.

4. **User-Centric Approach:** Like Google's other co-founder, Sergey Brin, Page places a significant emphasis on the user experience. He believes that focusing on creating the best user experience ultimately leads to success.

5. **Importance of Speed and Efficiency:** Page believes that speed is a significant factor in any competition, indicating that efficiency and the ability to act quickly can be decisive in business success.

6. **Dare to Dream:** From self-driving cars to balloon-powered internet, Larry Page has always aimed high. His career demonstrates the power of dreaming big and following through with action.

Remember, these takeaways are based on public knowledge of Page's actions and publicly stated views. They should be viewed as potential sources of inspiration, not as specific advice. Different strategies work for different people and situations.

Building a Media Empire through Authenticity and Resilience:

1. **Authenticity:** Oprah Winfrey has always been true to herself on screen and off. She built her brand on honesty and authenticity, which resonated with her audience and built trust.

2. **Empathy:** Winfrey is well-known for her empathetic interviewing style. Her ability to connect with people on a deep, personal level has been a major factor in her success.

3. **Overcoming Adversity:** Winfrey's personal story of overcoming adversity and trauma has served as an inspiration to millions. She reminds us of the power of resilience and determination.

4. **Lifelong Learning:** Winfrey is a firm believer in the power of education and lifelong learning. Her passion for knowledge has not only broadened her worldview but also allowed her to connect with a wide range of individuals.

5. **Use Success to Lift Others:** Through the Oprah Winfrey Leadership Academy for Girls and other philanthropic efforts, Winfrey has used her success to create opportunities for others, underscoring the importance of giving back.

6. **Importance of Self-Care:** Winfrey has often spoken about the importance of taking care of

one's physical, mental, and emotional health, emphasizing the need for balance in life.

As with other figures, these takeaways are based on public knowledge of Winfrey's actions, statements, and general understanding of her approach to life and work. They serve as potential points of inspiration, not as specific advice, as different strategies work for different people and situations.

Mastering the Art of Luxury and Brand Building:

1. **The Power of Branding:** Arnault's success with LVMH (Louis Vuitton Moët Hennessy) underlines the importance of branding and the value it can bring to a business.

2. **Commitment to Quality:** Arnault places significant emphasis on maintaining the highest quality for all LVMH products, reinforcing the idea that commitment to quality can differentiate a business.

3. **Strategic Acquisitions:** Arnault has grown LVMH through strategic acquisitions, showing the importance of wise investment and expansion decisions in business growth.

4. **Understanding Consumer Desire:** Arnault's success in the luxury market underlines the importance of understanding consumer desires and effectively catering to them.

5. **Preserving Heritage While Innovating:** Despite owning some of the world's oldest luxury brands, Arnault has consistently pushed for innovation, demonstrating that it's possible to respect tradition while embracing change.

6. **Developing Talent:** Arnault believes in recruiting and nurturing talented individuals who can bring fresh perspectives and drive growth, showing the importance of talent management in business success.

Like the other figures, these takeaways are based on public knowledge of Arnault's actions, public statements, and general understanding of his approach to business. They are intended as points of inspiration, not as specific advice, as different strategies are suited to different individuals and situations.

Inspiring Paths to Success

Visionary Leadership: Visionary leaders like Bernard Arnault, Steve Jobs, and Jack Ma demonstrate the importance of having a clear vision and the ability to inspire others to achieve greatness.

Embracing Innovation: Successful individuals such as Mukesh Ambani, Tim Cook, and Sergey Brin understand the significance of embracing innovation and staying at the forefront of technological advancements.

Entrepreneurial Spirit: The entrepreneurial spirits of Jack Ma, Richard Branson, and Larry Ellison showcase the willingness to take risks, seize opportunities, and build empires from scratch.

Commitment to Excellence: Leaders like Bernard Arnault and Mary Barra exemplify the dedication to excellence, quality, and a relentless pursuit of perfection.

Long-Term Perspective: Indra Nooyi, Satya Nadella, and Sundar Pichai emphasize the importance of having a long-term perspective, sustainable growth, and strategic decision-making.

Philanthropic Values: Sheryl Sandberg and Mukesh Ambani remind us of the significance of giving back to society and using success to make a positive impact through philanthropy.

These collective takeaways reflect the diverse paths taken by these successful individuals, showcasing their unique qualities, values, and approaches to achieve remarkable success in their respective fields.

Unleashing Potential: Strategies for Business Expansion and Transformation

Diversified Business Empire: Mukesh Ambani, Bernard Arnault, and Richard Branson exemplify the ability to build diversified business empires, expanding into multiple sectors and leveraging opportunities for growth.

Strategic Investments: Mukesh Ambani and Larry Ellison demonstrate the importance of strategic investments in positioning companies for future success and seizing new opportunities.

Embracing Technology: Mukesh Ambani, Satya Nadella, and Sundar Pichai highlight the transformative power of technology and the need to embrace it to drive innovation and growth.

Disruptive Leadership: Mukesh Ambani and Jack Ma showcase the ability to disrupt industries and challenge conventional norms, creating new possibilities for businesses.

Forward-Thinking Approach: Mukesh Ambani, Satya Nadella, and Sundar Pichai emphasize the importance of a forward-thinking mindset, focusing on emerging technologies and future trends.

Social Impact: Mukesh Ambani's and Richard Branson's commitment to philanthropy and societal development reminds us of the significance of using success to make a positive impact on communities.

Innovation and Empowerment: Pioneering Growth in the Digital Era

E-commerce Revolution: Jack Ma, the Architect of Digital Commerce, revolutionized the e-commerce landscape, demonstrating the power of digital platforms and enabling small businesses to thrive in the digital era.

Visionary Innovation: Steve Jobs and Larry Ellison exemplify the ability to envision and bring to life groundbreaking innovations that reshape industries and capture the imagination of consumers.

Technology and Connectivity: Satya Nadella, Sundar Pichai, and Sergey Brin emphasize the transformative potential of technology, connectivity, and the internet in driving economic and social progress.

Empowering Entrepreneurship: Jack Ma's emphasis on empowering entrepreneurs and fostering an ecosystem that supports small businesses highlights the significance of nurturing entrepreneurship for economic growth.

Leadership and Collaboration: Sheryl Sandberg, as a Collaborative Leader, showcases the importance of effective leadership, teamwork, and collaboration in driving organizational success.

Adaptability and Resilience: The collective experiences of these individuals, including Jack Ma, Steve Jobs, and Larry Ellison, underscore the importance of adaptability, resilience, and the ability to navigate through challenges in the ever-changing business landscape.

Visionary Leadership and Legacy: Inspiring Innovation and Transformation

Visionary Thinking: Steve Jobs, as a Visionary Trailblazer, exemplified the power of visionary thinking, challenging the status quo, and revolutionizing industries with groundbreaking products.

User-Centric Design: Tim Cook's focus on User-Centric Innovation highlights the importance of understanding and meeting the needs of customers, ensuring exceptional user experiences.

Continuity and Adaptation: Tim Cook's leadership as the Torchbearer of Apple's Legacy demonstrates the significance of continuity, while also adapting to changing market dynamics and technological advancements.

Design and Aesthetics: Steve Jobs and Jony Ive's collaboration showcased the importance of Design Excellence and meticulous attention to detail, creating iconic products that marry form and function.

Operational Efficiency: Tim Cook's expertise in Operations and Supply Chain Management enabled Apple to achieve operational excellence and ensure smooth product delivery to global markets.

Culture of Innovation: The collective efforts of Steve Jobs and Tim Cook fostered a Culture of Innovation within Apple, encouraging creativity, collaboration, and a relentless pursuit of excellence.

Leadership and Impact: Driving Success through Vision and Resilience

Transformational Leadership: Indra Nooyi, as a Transformation Catalyst, demonstrated the power of visionary leadership in driving organizational change and long-term success.

Strategic Decision-making: Indra Nooyi's strategic decision-making skills enabled PepsiCo to navigate through challenges and capitalize on emerging market trends.

Diversity and Inclusion: Indra Nooyi's emphasis on Diversity and Inclusion highlights the importance of fostering an inclusive culture that embraces diverse perspectives and values equality.

Branding and Innovation: Indra Nooyi's focus on brand building and product innovation enabled PepsiCo to maintain a competitive edge and expand its product portfolio.

Sustainable Business Practices: Indra Nooyi's commitment to sustainability and corporate social responsibility showcases the significance of integrating environmental and social considerations into business strategies.

Leadership Legacy: Tim Cook's leadership as the Successor Steward at Apple exemplifies the ability to maintain and build upon the legacy of a visionary leader, ensuring continuity and sustained success.

Innovation and Transformation: Leading with Purpose and Vision

1. Transformational Leadership: Satya Nadella, as a Transformation Catalyst, demonstrated the power of visionary leadership in driving Microsoft's transformation and embracing a growth mindset.
2. Cloud Computing and AI: Satya Nadella's focus on Cloud Computing and Artificial Intelligence (AI) enabled Microsoft to position itself as a leader in these transformative technologies.
3. Inclusive Culture: Satya Nadella's commitment to fostering an Inclusive Culture emphasizes the importance of diversity, empathy, and inclusivity in driving innovation and creating a positive work environment.
4. Purpose-driven Approach: Satya Nadella's purpose-driven approach at Microsoft emphasizes the significance of aligning business goals with social impact, promoting sustainability, and making a difference in society.
5. Collaborative Partnerships: Satya Nadella's emphasis on building Collaborative Partnerships and strategic alliances highlights the value of cooperation and leveraging the strengths of others to drive success.
6. Continuous Learning and Adaptation: Satya Nadella's belief in Continuous Learning and Adaptation underscores the need for individuals and organizations to embrace change, stay agile, and continuously evolve in the fast-paced tech industry.

Embracing Customer Obsession and Long-Term Thinking

1. **Customer Obsession:** Bezos built Amazon around the principle of customer obsession. He believed that focusing on what customers want, even when they can't articulate it themselves, is the key to success.

2. **Long-term Thinking:** Bezos often talks about the importance of long-term thinking. He believes in making decisions based on where you want to be years down the line, not just in the short term.

3. **Willingness to Invent and Pioneer:** Bezos emphasizes the importance of innovation and trying new things. He's not afraid to fail, viewing it as an essential part of invention and innovation.

4. **Embrace Change:** Bezos believes that being adaptable and open to change is crucial in a rapidly evolving business landscape.

5. **High Standards Across the Board:** He believes that high standards are teachable and contagious. By setting high standards, organizations can consistently deliver high-quality products, services, and processes.

Driving Innovation and Embracing

1. **Bold Vision:** Elon Musk is known for setting audacious goals and visions, such as colonizing Mars or transitioning the world to sustainable energy. This boldness can serve as inspiration for thinking big and aiming high.

2. **Embrace Failure:** Musk sees failure as an opportunity to learn and improve. This mindset fosters innovation and resilience, encouraging continual growth and development.

3. **Work Ethic:** Musk is renowned for his incredible work ethic. While this approach might not be sustainable for everyone, it underlines the importance of dedication and commitment to your goals.

4. **Cross-disciplinary Thinking:** Musk applies knowledge from different fields to solve problems. For example, his background in physics often informs his approach to engineering and business challenges.

5. **Take Risks:** Musk is not afraid to take risks. This willingness to venture into uncharted territory has enabled him to innovate and achieve groundbreaking successes.

6. **Constant Learning:** Musk emphasizes the importance of continual learning and growth. He reads extensively and is always open to new ideas and perspectives.

Unconventional Strategies for Overcoming Adversity

1. The Boathouse Fire: The author recounts the story of a boathouse fire that threatened to destroy everything the owner had worked towards. Faced with the imminent loss of his prized boats, the owner made a difficult decision to sink one of the boats to protect the rest. This act symbolizes the unconventional strategies one may need to employ when faced with seemingly insurmountable challenges.

2. Embracing Unconventional Solutions: When traditional approaches fail, it is important to think outside the box and consider alternative solutions. Sometimes, sinking a boat can be a metaphor for sacrificing a part of something in order to save the whole. This mindset encourages individuals to explore innovative and unexpected paths to overcome obstacles.

3. Infinite Capacity to Figure It Out: The author emphasizes the belief in one's unlimited capacity to find solutions. When pushed to their limits and faced with dire circumstances, individuals possess the resilience and resourcefulness to navigate challenges and discover a way forward.

4. Overcoming Adversity: Life is filled with unforeseen challenges and setbacks. It is during these moments that individuals are tested and must tap into their inner strength and creativity. Rather than succumbing to

defeat, they can embrace the opportunity to find unconventional solutions and rise above adversity.

5. Trusting Your Problem-Solving Abilities: The story of sinking the boat exemplifies the power of trusting one's instincts and problem-solving abilities. When faced with difficult choices, individuals can rely on their inner wisdom and make decisions that may seem counterintuitive but ultimately lead to a positive outcome.

6. Resilience and Adaptability: The ability to adapt and respond to unexpected situations is crucial. The boathouse owner's decision to sink the boat demonstrates adaptability and resilience in the face of adversity. It serves as a reminder that sometimes sacrifices need to be made in order to protect what truly matters.

7. Thinking Beyond Conventional Wisdom: Challenging times call for innovative thinking. The story encourages individuals to question conventional wisdom and explore alternative approaches to problem-solving. It inspires a mindset of curiosity and experimentation to find unique solutions.

All In: Embracing Risk and Commitment for Unprecedented Success

1. From Humble Beginnings to Success: The author reflects on his journey from a challenging upbringing to achieving success as a host of a TV show and an influential figure in the business world. His experiences highlight the transformative power of determination and unwavering commitment.

2. The Power of Going All In: Going all in means fully committing to a goal or endeavor without any backup plans or the possibility of turning back. It requires embracing risk and pushing forward with unwavering determination, trusting in one's instincts and capabilities.

3. Abandoning the Safety Net: Conventional wisdom often encourages the creation of backup plans and safety nets, but the author argues that relying on these safety nets can hinder success. By discarding Plan B and eliminating the option to lose, individuals can tap into their full potential and achieve greatness.

4. Trusting Your Instincts: In a world filled with external guidance and conventional wisdom, trusting one's instincts is crucial. The author emphasizes the importance of reconnecting with primal instincts and listening to one's inner voice when making bold decisions and pursuing ambitious goals.

5. Overcoming Doubt and Naysayers: Achieving greatness requires overcoming doubt, hesitation, and the negative influence of naysayers. By embracing a mindset of unwavering determination and blocking out negativity, individuals can persevere through challenges and achieve extraordinary results.

6. Victory Through Eliminating Failure: The author's journey demonstrates that victory can only be achieved by eliminating the option to fail. By fully committing to a goal and refusing to entertain the possibility of failure, individuals can unlock their full potential and achieve unprecedented success.

7. Equipping Others for Transformation: Through this book, the author aims to equip readers with the necessary tools and insights to embark on their own transformative journeys. By embracing the philosophy of going all in, individuals can overcome obstacles, embrace risk, and achieve their highest aspirations.

Embracing Failure and Resilience: A Journey of Risk and Reinvention

1. Overcoming Challenging Beginnings: The author's journey from a challenging Parisian neighborhood to achieving success in various professional realms highlights the power of perseverance and determination. Through education and hard work, the author defied expectations and pursued a path of success.

2. Success in Unexpected Realms: While the author had envisioned a career in the business world, they also found success in unexpected realms. From working as a press secretary and contributing to the rebuilding efforts of iconic landmarks to appearing on TV shows and teaching at Harvard Business School, the author embraced diverse opportunities and leveraged their skills and experiences.

3. Facing Failures and Embracing Risks: The author's experience with Omnichannel Acquisition Corp. and the failed deal with Kin Insurance highlights the reality of setbacks and failures. Instead of retreating, the author chose to embrace greater risks and pursue new opportunities, demonstrating resilience and a willingness to learn from failure.

4. Trusting the Philosophy of Going All In: The author's philosophy of going all in encouraged them to trust that failure could lead to something greater. Rather than playing it safe,

the author embraced new challenges, seeking greater freedom, autonomy, and rewards.

5. Reinvention and Pursuit of Greater Rewards: By leaving behind previous roles and exploring new avenues, the author embraced reinvention and continued to go all in. This mindset allowed them to seek new opportunities, such as launching their own show, engaging in metaverse investments, and writing a book.

6. Resilience in the Face of Adversity: The author's battle with COVID-19 and double pneumonia served as a reminder of the unpredictable nature of life. Despite setbacks and challenges, the author's resilience and determination pushed them forward, ready to take on new ventures and opportunities.

7. Lessons in Perseverance and Risk-Taking: Through the author's experiences, readers can learn the importance of perseverance, embracing risks, and trusting in their abilities. Failures and setbacks are not the end but rather opportunities for growth, reinvention, and the pursuit of greater rewards.

Embracing a No-Turning-Back Mentality

1. Historical Significance: The concept of burning the boats as a strategy for success dates back to ancient times and can be found in various historical accounts. From Israelite armies to Sun Tzu and Jules César, leaders understood that eliminating escape routes and committing fully to a mission would inspire unwavering dedication and determination.

2. Modern Examples: The recent example of Volodymyr Zelensky, the president of Ukraine, rejecting evacuation plans in the face of Russian invasion, demonstrates the power of burning the boats as a symbol of unwavering commitment and defiance against overwhelming odds. The story of the Parisian Lions rugby team and their coach Pierre Dupont invoking the legend of Hernán Cortés showcases how the philosophy of going all in can unlock untapped potential and lead to remarkable victories.

3. Personal Journey: The author shares their personal story of growing up in poverty and facing numerous challenges, highlighting the importance of embracing the philosophy of burning the boats. They credit their success to recognizing that they had to take full responsibility for their own life and future, refusing to wait for external support or guidance.

4. Trusting Instincts and Taking Action: The author emphasizes the significance of trusting one's instincts and taking decisive action. They highlight the detrimental impact of hesitation and the need to eliminate distractions and safety nets that may hinder progress and dilute focus.

5. Ownership and Self-Reliance: The author observes a common pattern among successful individuals and businesses—they understand that their success ultimately depends on their own efforts and decisions. They emphasize the importance of disregarding others' opinions and taking full ownership of one's journey.

6. Overcoming Hopelessness: The author's personal experience of growing up without hope, witnessing their mother's decline, and facing the challenges of their neighborhood fuels their belief in the power of embracing a no-turning-back mentality. They encourage readers to reject a victim mindset and seize control of their own lives.

7. Importance of Trust and Action: In the upcoming chapters, the author promises to delve deeper into the significance of trusting one's instincts and taking action. They emphasize that hesitation can hinder progress and that speed, guided by trust and determination, is more conducive to achieving dreams.

Embracing Risk and Trusting Your Instincts

1. Challenging Stereotypes: The author defies stereotypes associated with high school dropouts, emphasizing that their decision was not a result of failure or lack of motivation. Instead, it was a calculated plan driven by a vision for a better future and a deep trust in their instincts.

2. The Power of Instincts: Trusting one's instincts and pursuing opportunities before having all the evidence is a key aspect of breakout success. The author argues that abundant choices and backup plans can lead to paralysis, while embracing uncertainty and going all in can collapse the time delay between insight and action, leading to exponential returns.

3. Section Structure: The book is divided into three sections: "Take The Plunge" (Part One), "No Turning Back" (Part Two), and "Stack It Up" (Part Three). Each section explores a set of principles supported by personal anecdotes, company experiences, and relevant research, guiding readers toward tearing down barriers and living the life they're meant to live.

4. Overcoming Adversity: The author shares their challenging upbringing, including financial struggles and their mother's illness. Despite these obstacles, they refused to succumb to hopelessness and instead sought opportunities to improve their circumstances.

5. Inspiring Acts of Kindness: The author recounts the generosity of a local priest who provided food for their family during difficult times. This act of compassion left a lasting impact, reminding them of the power of love and support in times of need.

6. Embracing Responsibility: The author acknowledges that their success is a result of recognizing that no one else would pave the way for them. They took ownership of their own life and refused to wait for external guidance or support.

7. The Importance of Action: Hesitation and divided attention between goals and safety nets can hinder progress and limit success. The author highlights the significance of trusting instincts and taking decisive action, as hesitancy can kill dreams while speed leads to greater opportunities.

Trust Your Instincts: Embracing Self-Reliance for Extraordinary Success

1. Challenging Conventional Wisdom: The author emphasizes the importance of trusting one's instincts and not succumbing to external pressures or societal expectations. They share their personal journey of defying conventional wisdom and following their own path, despite facing challenges and setbacks.

2. Recognizing Privilege: While acknowledging their own privileges as a white male, the author aims to broaden the perspective by sharing stories of entrepreneurs from diverse backgrounds. They highlight that regardless of one's starting point or background, the principle of going all in and trusting instincts remains applicable to everyone.

3. Embracing Personal Brilliance: The book encourages readers to recognize their unique brilliance and expertise in their own lives. By understanding that they are the foremost authority on their own experiences, readers can tap into their full potential and trust themselves to make extraordinary decisions.

4. Resisting External Influences: Society often conditions individuals to dismiss their instincts and rely on external authorities. The book encourages readers to resist this conditioning and trust their internal compass, recognizing the value of their own thoughts and insights.

5. The Power of Self-Reliance: Quoting Victor Hugo, the author emphasizes the significance of self-reliance and the inner spark of light that flashes across one's mind. By embracing this self-reliance, individuals can uncover their true potential and seize opportunities that may otherwise be missed.

6. Overcoming Hesitation: Hesitation can be a barrier to realizing one's potential. The book inspires readers to overcome hesitation and take decisive action, even when their instincts don't align with societal expectations or conventional wisdom.

The Power of Vision: Unlocking Potential and Creating Extraordinary Outcomes

1. Defining Your Destination: The book emphasizes the importance of having a clear vision and defined goals. It encourages readers to identify their aspirations, dreams, and unique perspectives, as these are the building blocks for creating a path towards success.

2. Trusting Your Instincts: Examples of entrepreneurs like Emilie Harrel and Bernard Chevalier highlight the significance of trusting one's instincts and pursuing their visions, even when faced with skepticism or doubts from others. The book emphasizes the value of taking action and believing in one's ideas, as inaction can often result in missed opportunities.

3. Challenging the Status Quo: The story of Stéphane Rousseau's ambitious redevelopment project, Hudson Yards, demonstrates the power of seeing potential where others see obstacles. By challenging conventional wisdom and envisioning a new neighborhood from scratch, Stéphane was able to transform a neglected area into a vibrant, multi-purpose community.

4. Overcoming Challenges: Pursuing a vision often involves overcoming obstacles, such as financial crises, complex engineering challenges, and societal resistance. The book emphasizes the importance of perseverance,

resilience, and the ability to adapt in the face of adversity.

5. The Impact of Crystal-Clear Vision: Having a clear vision is crucial for success. Stéphane Rousseau's unwavering vision for Hudson Yards served as a guiding force that propelled the project forward, overcoming various hurdles and leading to its ultimate success.

6. Personalizing Your Vision: The book encourages readers to recognize their unique perspectives, talents, and gifts, and to infuse their vision with their own personal touch. It highlights that the best dreams are those that align with an individual's innermost desires, values, and strengths.

The Power of Intuition: Harnessing Insights and Trusting Your Instincts

1. The Value of Intrinsic Motivation: The book highlights the importance of personal experiences and intrinsic motivations as powerful drivers of vision and innovation. Examples such as Chloé Tremblay, Léa Dubois, and Sophie Martin demonstrate how tapping into personal passions and convictions can fuel transformative ideas.

2. Cumulative Experiences: Thomas Remy's journey of finding hidden value in overlooked places emphasizes the significance of cumulative experiences. The book encourages readers to draw upon their past encounters and knowledge to uncover opportunities and insights that others may have missed.

3. Gut Feelings and Intuition: The book emphasizes the role of intuition in decision-making and visionary thinking. Examples of leaders like Katrina Lake and Jeff Bezos showcase how combining data-driven insights with gut feelings can lead to breakthrough ideas and entrepreneurial success.

4. Trusting Your Vision: While data and external opinions have their place, the book encourages readers to trust their own vision and instincts. It emphasizes the need for introspection, asking challenging questions, and listening to inner voices to recognize unique insights and possibilities.

5. Taking Calculated Risks: Following one's intuition often involves taking risks that may not be fully supported by data or conventional wisdom. The book inspires readers to embrace risk and be willing to go beyond the known to pursue their vision. It highlights that true leaders and innovators dare to challenge the status quo and forge new paths based on their own unique perspectives.

6. The Power of Gut Sandwiches: Gut sandwiches, a metaphor for combining insights, intuition, and understanding human needs, are depicted as the driving force behind game-changing decisions. The book encourages readers to leverage their holistic understanding and gut instincts to drive innovation and create breakthrough ideas.

Leaps of Faith

1. Building Confidence in Your Instincts: Trusting your instincts is a skill that can be developed over time. Each decision based on gut feelings strengthens your intuition and builds confidence in your ability to make impactful choices. Just like successful entrepreneurs Kevin O'Leary and Lori Greiner, continually pushing yourself to explore new opportunities and industries leads to growth and learning.

2. Balancing Data and Gut Feelings: While data has its place, solely relying on it can lead to missed opportunities and second-guessing. Following the examples of Sean Harper and the founders of LOLA, recognizing the value of gut feelings and not dismissing them is crucial. Intuition provides a unique perspective that data alone cannot capture.

3. Overcoming Obstacles and Defying Expectations: Trusting your instincts involves making calculated moves and pursuing your goals despite doubts and obstacles. Like the author's own journey of pursuing a law degree while working and seeking higher positions, refusing to let past circumstances define you and believing in your ability to overcome challenges is vital.

4. Continuous Process of Trusting Instincts: Trusting your instincts is an ongoing process that requires self-reflection, self-awareness,

and the willingness to take calculated risks. By embracing your own vision and listening to your gut, you develop a stronger sense of direction and the confidence to make bold choices that lead to extraordinary outcomes.

5. Taking Control of Your Destiny: Being in the driver's seat of your life means recognizing when you're being held back or exploited and refusing to wait for recognition or pity. Time is limited, and the law of compound interest applies not only to money but also to ideas and achievements. Starting early and making progress sets you on a path to exponential growth and rewards.

6. Leaping into Opportunities: Taking leaps and risks is a common theme among successful individuals, as exemplified by Jason Feldman, CEO of Vault Health. Embracing opportunities and being open to change can lead to significant breakthroughs. When COVID-19 hit, Feldman pivoted the company's focus, highlighting the importance of adapting and seizing opportunities even in challenging times.

Navigating Challenges and Seizing Opportunities

1. Embracing Career Pivots: Jason's career journey, marked by industry shifts and adaptability, highlights the importance of embracing new opportunities and building a diverse skill set. Each experience contributes to your toolkit of skills and prepares you for future challenges.

2. Navigating Uncertain Situations: In times of crisis, such as the pandemic, those who are willing to jump in, figure things out, and pursue opportunities can make a significant impact. Trusting your instincts, being adaptable, and building resilience are essential qualities for navigating uncertainty and achieving success.

3. Shaping Your Future: Recognize that you have the power to shape your own future. Embrace a proactive mindset, take calculated risks, and seize opportunities when they arise. It is through action and determination that you can create a fulfilling and successful life.

4. The Importance of Taking Advantage of Opportunities: Opportunities are not unlimited, and recognizing and seizing openings is crucial. Accepting the challenge of becoming the youngest press secretary in French history was a defining moment for the author, envisioning it as a path to professional security and a way to transcend his

background. Taking advantage of opportunities can shape your narrative and propel you towards a better future.

5. Trusting Your Instincts During Adversity: Even when things fall apart, your instincts can guide you. The author's first day on the job as press secretary coincided with his mother's deteriorating health, financial struggles, and overwhelming pressure. Trusting his instincts, he pushed forward, driven by the belief that the new appointment would be his lifeboat.

6. Persistence in the Face of Challenges: Challenges and setbacks are part of the journey. The author's story did not unfold as expected, but the importance of trusting your instincts and persisting through difficult times remains. Instincts can guide you even when circumstances seem dire, and they can serve as a source of strength and resilience.

Trusting your instincts, embracing career pivots, navigating uncertainty, seizing opportunities, and persevering through challenges are key elements of personal and professional growth.

Embracing Resilience: Trusting Instincts in the Face of Adversity

1. Unexpected Tragedy: The author recounts the heartbreaking moment when his mother passed away, leaving him with a sense of relief and regret. In times of crisis, it is natural to yearn for someone else to take charge, but it is important to trust your instincts and take action, even when circumstances are overwhelming.

2. Kaley's Journey: Kaley's story exemplifies the power of resilience and determination in the face of unimaginable tragedy. Despite the loss of her father, she chose to continue his legacy and rebuild their family business. By embracing her instincts, she transformed her pain into fuel for growth and used her adversity as a catalyst for positive change.

3. Trusting Resilience: Adversity can test our character, but it is during these challenging times that our true strength shines through. Kaley's decision to trust her resilience and push forward serves as a reminder that we have the power to choose how we respond to difficult circumstances. Trusting our instincts and embracing resilience can lead to personal growth and a brighter future.

4. Overcoming Dark Times: Life often deviates from our plans, and we may face profound losses and seemingly insurmountable challenges. However, it is in these darkest

moments that our true character is revealed. By trusting our instincts, pushing forward, and using adversity as a source of strength, we can find a way to overcome even the most difficult times.

5. Creating a Better Future: Kaley's determination to rebuild her family's business not only allowed her to support herself and her siblings but also provided a platform to make a difference in the lives of others affected by cancer. Her story serves as a powerful reminder that by embracing resilience and trusting our instincts, we can create a better future for ourselves and impact the lives of those around us.

Overcoming Doubt and Achieving Greatness

1. Defining Our Own Identity: Our circumstances do not define us; it is the decisions we make and the actions we take that shape our lives. Regardless of the hardships we face, we have the power to create a better future for ourselves and make a positive impact on the lives of others.

2. Confronting Self-Doubt: Self-doubt can hinder our progress and erode our self-esteem. To succeed, we must cultivate unwavering confidence in ourselves and shed the fear of external and internal forces that seek to undermine our worth. Recognize that we are deserving of success and capable of achieving greatness.

3. Overcoming Limiting Beliefs: We need to confront and overcome the doubts that plague our minds. Silence the critical voices within and learn from our mistakes without letting them define us. Practicing self-compassion and embracing our vulnerabilities allows us to create a supportive environment for personal growth.

4. Embracing Humanity and Seeking Support: True strength lies in embracing our humanity and acknowledging our limitations. It takes courage to seek help when needed and practice self-care. By setting healthy boundaries and

seeking support, we sustain our well-being and
resilience on the journey to success.

5. Nurturing Self-Confidence: Believing in our
    own worthiness and potential is essential to
    overcoming the past and preparing for an
    unlimited future. Reject the notion that we are
    not enough and embrace the belief that we
    have the capacity to achieve greatness. Nurture
    self-confidence, show self-compassion, and
    embark on a path towards lasting success.

Pioneering Change

1. Embracing Skepticism as an Opportunity: Rather than dismissing naysayers, it is valuable to listen to their concerns and use them as an opportunity for reflection and improvement. Understanding and addressing doubts can help refine plans and make a vision more convincing to others.

2. Perseverance and Improvement: Overcoming obstacles requires tireless effort and a focus on continuous improvement. Nicholas and his team dedicated themselves to refining their technology, enhancing the user experience, and aligning their product with emerging trends and communities.

3. Recognizing Pre-Revenue Potential: Success is not always tied to immediate revenue. Investing in visionary ideas often requires a leap of faith and an understanding that traditional metrics may not apply in the early stages. Calculated risks can lead to significant breakthroughs.

4. Trusting Instincts and Seeing Beyond Doubt: Successful entrepreneurs like Dave Chang and Nicholas Horbaczewski trust their instincts and see beyond skepticism and doubt. Being immersed in their industries gives them unique insights and a deep understanding of emerging trends, enabling them to seize opportunities others may overlook.

5. Challenging the Status Quo: Success often involves challenging existing norms and embracing change. Believing in one's own ideas, taking action, and persevering through challenges and criticism can lead to groundbreaking achievements and lasting impact.

6. Perspectives and Bias: Critics and detractors may lack the necessary information or context to fully grasp a vision. Their perspectives and biases can hinder their ability to see the bigger picture and recognize the potential for change. It is important to remain steadfast in one's convictions and communicate the vision effectively.

7. Balancing Conflicting Expectations: Projects like the 9/11 Memorial highlight the need to navigate conflicting opinions and expectations. Considering alternative designs and approaches, while addressing diverse viewpoints, allows for the creation of a more inclusive and impactful outcome.

Navigating Criticism, Staying True to Vision, and Embracing Empathy

1. Learning from Memorial Sites: Drawing inspiration from other memorial sites, such as the Vietnam Veterans Memorial, can provide valuable insights into creating emotionally resonant designs. Abstract and thought-provoking designs can transcend the literal and evoke profound understanding.

2. Balancing Reflection and Rebirth: Creating a memorial site requires striking a balance between honoring the victims and representing resilience and hope. It is essential to develop an overarching plan that encompasses the site's elements while considering diverse perspectives.

3. Being Misunderstood: Not everyone will understand or appreciate a vision in its entirety. Accepting the possibility of being misunderstood in the present and trusting that history will judge the work can provide peace of mind.

4. Transforming Criticism into Opportunity: Criticism can be viewed as an opportunity to challenge assumptions, refine thinking, and strengthen resolve. It tests the merits of ideas and highlights the potential for increased rewards in taking risks and being a trailblazer.

5. Responding to Hate and Negativity: Instead of letting hate and negativity stick, having

empathy for critics can help understand their motivations. Recognizing that their criticism often stems from their own insecurities and limitations allows for a more compassionate response.

6. Staying True to Vision: Remaining steadfast in one's vision and not letting compromised opinions sway decisions is crucial. Understanding that criticism can be driven by envy, discomfort with change, or fear of exposure helps maintain focus and resilience.

7. Embracing Self-Reflection and Improvement: Viewing criticism as an opportunity for self-reflection and improvement allows for growth. Challenging assumptions, refining thinking, and defending the merits of ideas help navigate through criticism.

Embracing Self-Belief: Overcoming Doubts and Critics

1. Define Your Own Worth: Your past does not define your potential or limit your future. Embrace the power to shape your own narrative and believe in your abilities.
2. Trust Your Instincts: Follow your inner voice and trust your gut feelings. Sometimes the greatest opportunities lie where others fail to see them.
3. Embrace Discomfort and Challenge the Status Quo: Progress often requires stepping out of your comfort zone, pushing boundaries, and challenging the norms. Be willing to go against the grain and pursue unconventional paths.
4. Surround Yourself with Supportive Individuals: Seek out mentors, friends, and a supportive network who believe in your potential and uplift you. Their encouragement will help fuel your confidence and resilience.
5. Reframe Self-Doubt with Positive Self-Talk: Confront and challenge the negative voices in your mind. Use positive affirmations to reframe your thoughts and boost your self-belief.
6. Learn from Setbacks: View setbacks as opportunities for growth and learning. Embrace resilience and persevere through challenges, using them as stepping stones on your journey to success.
7. Stay True to Your Vision: The opinions of others should not define your worth or determine your path. Stay focused on your vision, trust your instincts, and remain steadfast in your pursuit of your goals.

Embracing Vulnerability: Triumph over Flaws and Stigma

1. Rewrite Your Narrative: Our past or flaws do not define us. Embrace the power to reframe your story and find strength in vulnerability.
2. Seek Support and Guidance: Surround yourself with friends, mentors, or professionals who can provide a fresh perspective and support during challenging times.
3. Find Humor and Humanity: Rather than letting shame or embarrassment consume you, find humor and humanity in your flaws. Embrace your imperfections as part of your unique journey.
4. Authenticity and Humility: Be true to yourself and acknowledge your struggles. By sharing your vulnerabilities, you can create meaningful connections and inspire others.
5. Triumph through Adversity: Overcoming personal struggles can lead to astonishing triumphs. Use your experiences as motivation to achieve greatness and defy expectations.
6. Celebrate Imperfections: Embrace your humanity, flaws, and insecurities. Recognize that they are part of what makes you unique and relatable.
7. Break Stigma and Inspire Others: By sharing your own journey and challenging societal stigmas, you can create a positive impact, provide hope, and encourage others to seek support and understanding.

From Incarceration to Inspiration: The Power of Turning Adversity into Art

1. Discovering Passion in Unexpected Places: Isaac Wright found his passion for photography while serving in the army, demonstrating that inspiration can arise in the most unlikely circumstances.
2. Embracing Fearless Pursuit: Isaac fearlessly pursued his passion, scaling heights and pushing boundaries to capture unique and awe-inspiring images. He refused to let fear hold him back from his creative vision.
3. Transforming Setbacks into Stepping Stones: Despite facing legal trouble and incarceration, Isaac saw his time in jail as a test of resilience. He maintained his belief in his art and used his circumstances as motivation to persevere.
4. Unwavering Self-Belief: Throughout his journey, Isaac unwaveringly believed in his own greatness and the transformative power of his art. He used this self-belief to fuel his determination and overcome obstacles.
5. Impacting the World: Isaac's story of triumph resonates beyond his personal success. He committed a significant portion of his earnings to support the Bail Project, demonstrating his commitment to making a positive impact on the lives of others.
6. Inspiring Possibility: Through his art, Isaac aimed to expand human consciousness and inspire others to recognize the vastness of what is possible. He shows us that even in the face of adversity, our dreams can lead us to unimaginable heights.

The Power of Resilience: Turning Setbacks into Stepping Stones

Embracing Adversity: Isaac's story inspires high school equivalency certificate students, showing them that their challenging backgrounds do not define their potential. Overcoming adversity can be an asset that showcases resilience and determination.

Rise from Challenging Circumstances: Isaac emphasizes that starting from a difficult place in life can make subsequent success even more remarkable. Students are encouraged to embrace their journeys and understand that their backgrounds can be sources of strength.

Surviving and Aspiring: Isaac admires individuals who not only survive but also continue to reach for more, striving to improve their lives despite hardships. The ability to pursue greater aspirations sets them apart.

Persistence and Forward Motion: Isaac's observations reveal that successful people share a common trait—the ability to persist and keep moving forward despite challenges and setbacks. It is this resilience that propels them towards success.

Failures as Opportunities: Michael Rubin's entrepreneurial journey exemplifies the mindset of seeing failures as stepping stones. Instead of letting setbacks define him, he viewed them as invaluable opportunities for growth and learning.

Redefining Success: High achievers understand that failures are part of the journey towards greatness. They extract valuable lessons from setbacks and expand their definition of success to accommodate the failures along the way.

Embracing Failure, Cultivating Empathy: Keys to Personal and Professional Growth

Embracing Failure: Dave Chang encourages embracing failure as a natural part of pushing boundaries and striving for excellence. Processing failure involves acknowledging it, learning from it, and committing to future success.

Overcoming Loss Aversion: Understanding the psychological bias of loss aversion allows individuals to focus on potential gains and take calculated risks. High achievers rewire their mindset to care less about losses and embrace the possibilities for success.

Celebrating Risk-Taking: Celebrating the act of calculated risk-taking, regardless of the outcome, is crucial. Failure is not the goal, but learning and growth are essential when setbacks occur.

Setbacks as Stepping Stones: Setbacks and failures are not permanent labels but opportunities for growth. Absorbing wins, reflecting on losses, and maintaining resilience are key to navigating challenges and achieving goals.

The Power of Empathy: Self-compassion and acceptance are crucial for personal and professional growth. Empathy towards ourselves and others creates a supportive work environment that fosters loyalty, resilience, and motivation.

Creating a Supportive Work Environment: Leaders who cultivate empathy and create space for healing and growth in the workplace foster a thriving atmosphere. Offering empathy and care motivates individuals to go the extra mile and bring their whole selves to work.

Embracing Mortality, Taking Risks: Stories of Living Fearlessly

Work-Life Balance and Intentional Choices: Success often requires periods of intense effort and recovery. It's important to be intentional in our choices, prioritize what truly matters, and make sacrifices to achieve extraordinary things.

Reflecting on Mortality: Acknowledging our mortality helps us overcome critics and focus on what truly matters. It reminds us that time is limited and precious, shifting our perspective to let go of unimportant things and live fearlessly in the present moment.

Seizing Opportunities and Dreaming Big: Embracing the impermanence of life gives us the courage to dream big and live fully. We must make the most of the precious gift of life we've been given and not waste our potential.

Recognizing Potential and Taking Leaps: Sometimes, others see our potential more clearly than we do ourselves. The support and belief of mentors and loved ones can empower us to take risks and pursue our true calling.

Building a Support System: Having a support system that believes in us is invaluable. Surrounding ourselves with mentors, partners, and friends who support our dreams and provide financial or emotional backing can give us the confidence to take bold steps.

Embracing Risks, Defying Doubts: Jesse Derris' Journey to Success

Recognizing Others' Insight: Sometimes, others can see our potential more clearly than we can. Embracing their belief in us and their vision for our future can propel us towards success.

Taking the Leap: Success requires taking risks and stepping out of our comfort zones. It's important to confront doubts and fears, trusting in our abilities and having control over our own destiny.

Embracing Setbacks and Mistakes: Setbacks, obstacles, and mistakes are part of the journey. It's crucial not to let them define us or deter us from pursuing our dreams. Embracing vulnerability and learning from challenges can lead to extraordinary achievements.

Inspiring Others: Achieving success can inspire and empower others. Becoming a mentor and guiding those who are hesitant to take their own leaps of faith can have a profound impact on others' lives.

Gratitude and Humility: Remaining grounded, grateful, and humble amidst success is essential. Recognizing the support of mentors, partners, and oneself helps maintain the resilience and belief needed to overcome doubts and continue pursuing dreams.

Embracing Change and Finding Fulfillment

Overcoming Fear of Wasted Time: It's important to confront the fear of wasted time and effort that may arise when considering a change in direction. Recognize that success is not solely defined by past investments, but by the choices made in the present and future.

Shifting Focus to Opportunities: Instead of dwelling on sunk costs, focus on the opportunities that lie ahead. Embrace the potential for growth and fulfillment in unfamiliar territories.

Discovering Purpose and Resonance: Sometimes, letting go of what we thought we wanted allows us to discover what truly resonates with us. Finding a sense of purpose and fulfillment often requires exploring new paths and embracing change.

Learning from Challenges: Challenges and uncertainties are part of the journey. Embrace them as valuable lessons that propel personal growth and development. The skills and resilience gained from past experiences can be applied to navigate new territories.

Following True Passions: Making the decision to leave a secure path and pursue true passions can lead to profound fulfillment. Trusting in oneself and charting a course aligned with personal passions can result in a rewarding and purposeful journey.

Letting Go of Sunk Costs

The Fallacy of Sunk Costs: The notion that we must continue investing in something solely because of the time, energy, or money already spent is a fallacy. It's important to recognize that true success lies in our willingness to adapt and pursue what brings us fulfillment, even if it means leaving behind past investments.

Embracing New Possibilities: Fear of the unknown should not hold us back from exploring new paths and trying new things. The greatest achievements often stem from the willingness to step outside our comfort zones and venture into uncharted territories.

The Value of Happiness and Excitement: Just as children should prioritize activities that bring them joy and excitement, adults should listen to their hearts and pursue endeavors that align with their true aspirations. Happiness and fulfillment should guide decision-making, even if it means deviating from the familiar.

Retaining Skills and Knowledge: Past experiences and acquired skills are never wasted. They shape us and provide a foundation for future endeavors. The lessons learned and knowledge gained can be applied in new and exciting ways, enhancing our success in future ventures.

Following One's True Path: It's essential to listen to our hearts and trust our instincts when it comes to making choices. Our investment in time, energy, or money should not overshadow our pursuit of a fulfilling and purposeful life. Choosing a different path can lead to incredible personal growth and triumphs.

Trusting Your Instincts and Seizing Opportunities: Lessons from Visionary Entrepreneurs

Identifying Opportunities: Successful entrepreneurs often spot opportunities where others may not. They observe market gaps, identify unmet needs, and envision innovative solutions to address them.

Trusting Your Instincts: Following your instincts and believing in your ideas is crucial, even if others don't initially understand or see the same opportunity. The two friends who created a new cereal and Marc Lore, the entrepreneur behind Diapers.com and Jet.com, trusted their instincts and pursued their visions despite skepticism.

Combining Nostalgia and Trends: Incorporating elements of nostalgia, like childhood cereals, with current trends, such as health-conscious eating, can lead to unique and appealing products. By combining different concepts, entrepreneurs can create something innovative and capture the attention of consumers.

Taking Calculated Risks: Successful entrepreneurs understand the importance of taking calculated risks. They carefully assess the potential rewards and weigh them against the potential risks. It's about finding the balance between creativity and practicality.

Execution and Adaptation: Having a great idea is just the first step. The ability to execute the idea and adapt to changing circumstances is crucial for long-term success. Entrepreneurs need to be flexible, open to feedback, and willing to make adjustments along the way.

Persistence and Resilience: Entrepreneurship is not without its challenges. Persistence, resilience, and a belief in one's vision are essential for overcoming obstacles and persevering through setbacks.

Embracing Unconventional Paths: Success often comes from thinking differently and making your own choices. Entrepreneurs like Marc Lore demonstrate that by challenging conventional norms and finding alternative approaches, incredible achievements can be realized.

Lessons in Entrepreneurship and Goal Achievement

Recognizing Opportunities: Successful entrepreneurs like Marc Lore have a unique ability to identify opportunities that others may overlook. They see potential in market gaps, customer needs, or untapped areas, and are willing to take risks to capitalize on them.

Execution and Determination: Having a great idea is just the beginning. Success comes from executing the idea effectively and being committed to making it work. Passion, determination, and a relentless pursuit of excellence are essential ingredients for achieving remarkable outcomes.

Unique Perspectives and Insights: Trusting your own observations and ideas is crucial. Everyone has a unique perspective, and recognizing the value of your proprietary insights can lead to significant achievements. Act on your insights promptly and don't wait for someone else to seize the opportunity.

Avoiding Backup Plans: Research suggests that creating backup plans can hinder your chances of achieving your primary goals. Having a backup plan can subconsciously diminish your motivation and focus, making you less committed to your main goal. Instead, channel your energy and efforts into executing your primary goal with unwavering determination.

Embracing Uncertainty and Challenging Goals: Pursuing ambitious goals often involves stepping out of your comfort zone and embracing uncertainty. Overcoming fear and embracing the unknown are essential for personal and professional growth. Trust in your abilities and believe in your capacity to navigate challenges along the way.

Execution Matters: Success isn't solely about having completely new ideas; it's about how you execute those ideas. Pay attention to the details, the customer experience, and the value you provide. Even a small twist or improvement on an existing concept can lead to remarkable success if executed with excellence.

Persistence and Adaptation: Entrepreneurship and goal achievement require persistence, resilience, and adaptability. Be prepared to face setbacks, learn from failures, and make adjustments along the way. Embrace a growth mindset that sees challenges as opportunities for growth and improvement.

Power of Commitment

The Pitfalls of Backup Plans: While having a backup plan may provide a sense of security, it can divide your focus and diminish your commitment to your main goal. By going all-in and eliminating the distractions of a backup plan, you increase your chances of success.

Burning the Boats: Commit fully to your goals and dreams without the safety net of alternative options. Dedicate your energy and focus to your primary objective, giving it your best effort without doubt or reservation.

Trust in Your Abilities: Instead of doubting yourself, have confidence in your skills and capabilities. Believe that you have what it takes to achieve your goals and overcome challenges along the way.

Embracing Discomfort and Stress: Introduce controlled discomfort and stress into your practice or preparation to build resilience and thrive in high-pressure situations. By exposing yourself to challenging environments, you can develop the skills to perform at your best when it truly counts.

Effective Stress Management: Learning to manage stress and discomfort effectively is crucial. Develop strategies to regulate your emotions, enhance situational awareness, and adapt to changing circumstances. This enables you to perform at a high level even in the face of adversity.

Letting Go of Security for True Passion: Sometimes, letting go of a secure and comfortable situation is necessary to pursue your true dreams and make a meaningful impact. Trust your instincts and take risks to reach your full potential.

Attention to Detail and Continuous Improvement: Paying attention to detail and continuously seeking improvement can make a significant difference in your performance and success. Embrace a growth mindset and constantly strive to enhance your skills and knowledge.

Overcoming Circumstances, Pursuing Dreams, and Creating Opportunities

Embracing Stress for Peak Performance: The Yerkes-Dodson law suggests that an optimal level of stress or anxiety can enhance performance. Eric Mangini's approach to managing stress in training sessions aimed to find the right balance to push players to perform at their best.

Accepting Personal Circumstances: Sometimes, external circumstances limit our options and opportunities. It's important to accept and understand these constraints while still seeking ways to pursue our dreams within the given parameters.

Self-Reflection and Desire for Validation: Reflecting on missed opportunities can create a sense of longing for validation and a desire to prove oneself. It's natural to yearn for recognition and a chance to showcase one's capabilities.

Identifying Unique Expertise: When seeking opportunities, identify areas where you have specialized knowledge or experiences that set you apart from others. Highlighting this expertise can help you stand out and create value in your chosen field.

Building Connections and Relationships: Cultivating strong connections and relationships is essential for creating opportunities. Matt's ability to demonstrate his network and relationships in the direct-to-consumer (DTC) space added value to his proposal for teaching at Harvard Business School.

Belief in Yourself: Believe in your abilities and be persistent in pursuing your dreams. Even in the face of challenges and initial skepticism, maintaining confidence and determination can lead to remarkable opportunities.

Collaboration and Mentorship: Having a mentor or someone who believes in your potential can significantly impact your journey. Len Schlesinger's belief in Matt's vision and his willingness to co-teach the class at Harvard Business School demonstrates the power of collaboration and support.

Embracing Discomfort and Pursuing Meaningful Goals: Lessons from Samantha's Journey

1. Aligning Goals with Personal Values: Samantha and her partner chose to forego a traditional wedding and use their savings to start their own business because they felt it would be more fulfilling and help them move forward in their lives and careers. It's important to evaluate our goals and ensure they align with our values and aspirations, rather than pursuing them solely for external validation or societal expectations.

2. Sacrificing for Meaningful Outcomes: Samantha and her partner were willing to make sacrifices, such as canceling a planned vacation and postponing purchasing a home, in order to dedicate themselves fully to their goal. They recognized that achieving meaningful outcomes often requires short-term sacrifices and a strong commitment to hard work and perseverance.

3. Adapting to Unexpected Challenges: When their initial plan of renting out their house through Airbnb was disrupted by the COVID-19 pandemic, Samantha and her partner adapted and moved into the house themselves. They remained flexible and open to new opportunities, which eventually led them to sell the house at a profit and embark on a new venture. Being adaptable and finding creative

solutions in the face of challenges is crucial for success.

4. Evaluating Feasibility and Skills: Samantha's earlier experience with Leap Seats taught her the importance of being realistic about the feasibility of a business idea and considering the necessary skills and resources. It's essential to thoroughly evaluate the viability of our plans, consider potential obstacles, and ensure we have the capabilities and foundation to support our goals.

5. Pursuing Goals for the Right Reasons: Samantha's story underscores the significance of pursuing goals for intrinsic reasons rather than external expectations or superficial motives. It's important to have a genuine desire for personal growth, fulfillment, and the positive impact our goals can have on our lives and the lives of others.

Bridging Gaps and Embracing Excellence

1. Identifying a Gap: Recognizing gaps in education or areas where practical experience is lacking can present unique opportunities. Matt and Len identified a gap in teaching about the direct-to-consumer (DTC) space at Harvard Business School, which led them to create a groundbreaking class.

2. Connecting Classroom and Real-World: By inviting founders of DTC businesses to share their insights and experiences with students, Matt and Len bridged the gap between traditional classroom learning and the rapidly evolving world of entrepreneurship. They aimed to provide students with a firsthand understanding of modern business practices.

3. Overcoming Challenges: Matt faced challenges and anxiety while preparing for the class. However, his determination, hard work, and commitment to excellence drove him to overcome these obstacles. He recognized that delivering an exceptional learning experience required going above and beyond.

4. Immersive Learning Experience: Matt and Len aimed to create an immersive and memorable learning experience for the students. By bringing in guest speakers and providing unique opportunities like working with NFL players or having breakfast with successful entrepreneurs, they created an environment

that engaged all the senses and left a lasting impact.

5. Going the Extra Mile: Matt's dedication to the class went beyond what was expected. He transformed his home into a mock classroom and put in countless hours of preparation and refining his teaching materials. His commitment to excellence demonstrated his determination to deliver something truly exceptional.

6. Proving Personal Potential: Matt's pursuit of teaching at Harvard Business School was not just about achieving external validation; it was also about proving his own potential for greatness. He recognized that settling for mediocrity was not an option if he wanted to push himself and achieve personal satisfaction.

Harnessing Its Power for Success and Growth

1. Fear can drive you to achieve great things. When you feel afraid or anxious about something, it can push you to work hard and add value. It can motivate you to do your best and prove yourself.

2. Making yourself indispensable is important for professional success. No matter how small or unimportant a task may seem, if someone trusts you with it, then it's important enough to do it well. By doing your best, even in seemingly menial tasks, you can show your value and make a positive impact.

3. Fear can be a powerful tool when channeled properly. It can push you to go beyond your limits and accomplish things you never thought possible. By using anxiety as motivation, you can achieve higher levels of success.

4. However, it's crucial not to let fear push you over the edge. Comedian Gary Gulman faced setbacks and battled anxiety and depression, which almost led him to give up on his career. Instead of succumbing to his fears, he channeled his anxiety into his work, creating a new show that received critical acclaim and took his career to new heights. It's important to find ways to overcome fear and use it to your advantage, rather than letting it hold you back.

5. Baseball pitcher Zack Greinke struggled with
    social anxiety, which affected his performance
    and made him question his love for the game.
    With the help of treatment, he found a way to
    manage his anxiety and continue his career.
    Despite the challenges he faced, Greinke has
    had an exceptional career and is considered
    one of the best pitchers in baseball.

Fear and Success: Navigating Anxiety, Preparation, and Self-Belief

1. Anxiety and fear can have both positive and negative effects. While fear can push you to achieve great things, it can also cross a threshold and hinder your performance. It's important to recognize when anxiety becomes overwhelming and derails your progress.

2. Fear and anxiety can manifest in different ways. The author shares their personal struggles with anxiety, insomnia, and obsessive worries. These challenges can affect productivity and success.

3. Preparation is crucial for managing anxiety. The author demonstrates their dedication to being prepared by watching every episode of a TV show, taking notes, and even focusing on physical appearance. Understanding yourself and your motivations is essential. Addressing concerns that might hold you back can help you feel ready to perform your best.

4. Even with thorough preparation, anxiety can still arise. The author describes feeling sleepless and anxious before a significant TV appearance. However, they find ways to ground themselves, drawing inspiration from past experiences and seeking advice from others.

5. Overcoming fear and trusting yourself is vital. In high-pressure situations, it's important to remind yourself that you belong there and have the skills to succeed. Embracing the challenge, taking a deep breath, and believing in your abilities can help you overcome fear and perform at your best.

Finding Reassurance: Research, Data, and Informed Decision-Making to Alleviate Anxiety

1. Finding reassurance through research and data can help alleviate anxiety. The author emphasizes the importance of seeking scientific evidence or studies that support your goals or actions. Understanding that others have been successful in similar situations can provide confidence and help overcome doubts.

2. The author shares a personal example of running a marathon in Paris after experiencing sleeplessness due to jet lag. By reaching out to a team doctor and conducting online research, the author found reassurance that physical performance can withstand sleep deprivation for a certain period. This knowledge helped boost their confidence and improve their marathon performance.

3. Not every situation will have readily available data or studies to support your efforts. However, the vast number of people in the world means that someone has likely experienced what you're going through. Finding stories or advice from individuals who have faced similar challenges can provide valuable insights and help you make informed decisions while reducing worry.

4. Relying on facts and informed decision-making can help alleviate anxiety and prevent the repetition of mistakes. By seeking

information and learning from others'
experiences, you can approach situations with
more confidence and overcome unnecessary
worry.

Empowering Well-being: Meditation, Self-Care, and Personalized Approaches to Success

1. Meditation is a powerful tool for relaxation and mental well-being. Many successful CEOs and individuals practice transcendental meditation to calm their minds and enhance various aspects of their lives. It has been shown to boost resilience, emotional intelligence, creativity, relationships, and focus. Incorporating meditation into your daily routine can be a valuable addition to your anxiety tool kit.

2. Self-care is essential for maintaining peak performance. Treating yourself well, including practicing self-care habits, is critical for professional success and overall well-being. It's important to prioritize self-care, even when things get busy, as denying yourself the gift of self-care can have negative effects on your life.

3. Developing good self-care habits and making them consistent can lead to long-term benefits. Starting small and being consistent in your self-care practices increases the likelihood of sticking to them over time. Forming these habits early on allows you to reap the rewards and make them a natural part of your routine.

4. While some people thrive on routines and removing decision points from their day, everyone approaches life differently. Find

what works best for you and supports your excellence. It's okay if routines don't suit your style or hinder your spontaneous insights. Experiment with different approaches and adapt them to your own preferences and needs.

5. Having the right person by your side can make a significant difference. A supportive partner who brings calmness, rationality, and complementary skills can be a valuable asset. They can act as a force multiplier, helping you unleash your full potential and providing support in challenging times.

6. It's important to find what works best for you and not compare yourself to others. While meditation and having the right partner are valuable, everyone's journey is unique. Try different approaches, forgive yourself when you don't achieve perfection, and continue exploring what works best for your personal growth and well-being.

Building Strong Partnerships: Value Alignment, Vulnerability, and Seeking Support for Success

1. Choosing the right partner is crucial for success. Contrary to the idea that opposites attract, similarity and value alignment often lead to more lasting and powerful partnerships. When selecting a personal or professional partner, it's important to have a shared vision of the future and common ideas about what's important. Value overlap and heading in the same direction are key factors in successful partnerships.

2. Pay attention to the strength of relationships when evaluating investments or partnerships. Observing how partners interact with each other can provide insights into the health and compatibility of the relationship. Signs of contempt or conflict may indicate trouble ahead. Look for unity, shared passion, and a sense of togetherness in partnerships, as these qualities often indicate a strong foundation.

3. Embrace vulnerability and seek help to address your weaknesses. Admitting weaknesses and asking for assistance can be challenging due to fear of judgment or negative consequences. However, exposing your vulnerabilities and seeking support is a simple but effective strategy for growth and improvement. Don't hesitate to reach out for help when needed.

4. Intensity and passion can be both strengths and weaknesses. While being highly committed and intense can drive success, it can also lead to negative consequences if not managed properly. Excessive intensity can manifest as anxiety and result in harmful behaviors. Recognize when intensity is becoming detrimental and seek professional help or intervention to address any issues that may arise.

5. Providing support and seeking professional help can make a significant difference. In the example of Mike Tannenbaum, getting him the necessary support from an industrial psychologist helped address the anxiety-driven intensity that could have jeopardized his success and career. Recognize when someone you care about may need assistance and encourage them to seek appropriate help.

Transformative Growth: Seeking Help, Embracing Ambition, and Balancing Intensity for Success

1. Seeking help and support can lead to self-awareness and personal growth. Mike Tannenbaum's experience of getting professional help provided him with valuable insights and made him more comfortable with his vulnerabilities. It allowed him to develop coping mechanisms and create a more conducive work environment that helped manage his intense emotions.

2. Imposter syndrome and a mix of ambition and insecurity can be both a blessing and a curse. Mike's drive to achieve greatness was influenced by his father's work ethic, but it also led to feelings of unworthiness and constant questioning of readiness. Recognizing these dynamics and finding healthier ways to express ambition and manage insecurities can lead to improved performance.

3. Balancing intensity and recognizing shades of gray. Mike acknowledges that his intensity can still be challenging to calibrate, but he understands the importance of not letting everything make him angry. Learning to navigate the nuances of different situations and embracing flexibility can lead to more balanced and effective responses.

4. Mike's continued success and growth demonstrate the power of asking for help and constantly striving to improve. He has excelled in various roles and platforms, leveraging his expertise and experiences to contribute to the field of football and mentor aspiring individuals. Embracing continuous learning and development is a key factor in long-term success.

Embracing Crises: Turning Challenges into Opportunities for Growth and Success

1. Embrace each crisis as an opportunity for growth and reaching new heights. Positive emotions during crises can lead to long-term resilience and increased coping abilities. By focusing on the positive and actively seeking moments of hope, gratitude, awe, and contentment, you can reframe uncomfortable situations and see them as opportunities for personal and professional development.

2. Foster a mindset of crisis management even in the absence of a crisis. A "Go all in" mindset harnesses the clarity and focus that comes during a crisis without needing an actual crisis to occur. It involves limiting choices, prioritizing what truly matters, and being willing to iterate, pivot, and take creative and flexible actions to save and grow your business.

3. Reframe your perspective on work and other aspects of life by substituting "have to" with "get to." Recognize the privilege and opportunity in the things you do, such as going to work, rather than seeing them as burdens. This shift in mindset can enhance gratitude and motivation.

4. Recognize that crisis management skills and the ability to navigate difficult situations can be developed through personal experiences, including past traumas. Overcoming

challenging circumstances can build resilience and provide you with the confidence that you can manage your way through anything.

By embracing crises, maintaining a crisis-ready mindset, and focusing on the positive, you can turn challenges into opportunities and navigate the unpredictable nature of the world with resilience and success.

Weathering the Storm: Navigating Crisis with Persistence and Determination

1. In any crisis, the first step is to focus on survival. Even when you don't have all the answers, show up and find ways to keep going. Persistence and a determination to find a way forward are key to weathering difficult situations and ensuring long-term viability.

2. Embrace the opportunity to demonstrate your values and make a positive impact during a crisis. Look beyond fear and seize the chance to live out your company's values, support your employees, and contribute to the greater good. By prioritizing your people and taking bold action, you can strengthen your business and build loyalty.

3. Face the worst-case scenario and create practical plans to overcome it. Imagine the full extent of the disaster and identify the steps and resources needed to survive and move forward. By envisioning yourself still standing after the worst has happened, you can alleviate fear and free your mind to focus on solutions.

4. Accept the possibility of a nightmare scenario but don't let it consume you. Take appropriate measures to protect yourself and your business, but don't let worry hinder your progress. Instead, reallocate your energy towards pursuing something bigger and use the excess mental capacity to drive growth and success.

Thriving in Crisis: Navigating Challenges and Driving Success

1. When faced with a crisis, ask yourself the question: If I were starting from scratch today, what would I do? This question helps you think outside the box and reimagine your approach. Milk Bar founder Christina Tosi's pivot during the COVID-19 pandemic is an example of embracing this mindset and finding new opportunities even in the midst of chaos.

2. Trust your instincts and leverage what you already have. Even in a crisis, you possess the answers and resources within you. Avoid getting overwhelmed by external voices and complexities. Focus on leveraging your strengths and finding innovative solutions.

3. Crisis management requires decisive action and adaptability. Make hard decisions to survive longer, pivot your business model to meet current needs, and lead from the front. Give yourself the freedom to act and don't let excessive checks and balances hinder your ability to follow your instincts and pursue exceptionalism.

4. Collaboration should serve a purpose and not be pursued solely for the sake of consensus. While input from others can be valuable, don't let it suffocate innovation. Stay true to your vision and be willing to abandon ideas that

don't align with your instincts, even if others don't see what you see.

5. Crisis extends beyond life-or-death situations; it also includes missed opportunities due to lack of autonomy or the freedom to execute change. Take ownership of your decisions and create an environment that allows for agility and action.

Seizing Opportunities in Crisis: Trusting Instincts, Taking Action, and Driving Change

1. When faced with a crisis, ask yourself: If I were starting from scratch today, what would I do? This question prompts you to think creatively and reimagine your approach. Look for new opportunities and pivot your strategy to meet the current needs of your customers.

2. Trust your instincts and leverage what you already have. In a crisis, you may be seeking answers externally, but remember that you already possess the resources and abilities within yourself. Trust your gut and find ways to leverage your existing strengths and capabilities.

3. Embrace the potential for new opportunities that a crisis brings. While crises can bring destruction, they also open doors to possibilities that may not have been realized otherwise. See the crisis as a catalyst for growth and seize the chance to create a stronger and more successful business.

4. Act decisively and lead from the front. In times of crisis, it's crucial to make tough decisions and take decisive actions to ensure the survival and success of your business. Be proactive, engage with your customers, inspire your team, and take charge of the situation.

5. Give yourself the freedom to act and trust your intuition. Avoid being encumbered by excessive approval processes or the need for consensus. In times of innovation, overreaching checks and balances can hinder success. Trust your instincts, follow your intuition, and have the autonomy to execute on your ideas.

Seizing the Moment: Taking Action on Epiphanies and Opportunities

1. Epiphanies and opportunities are not endless. When you have a moment of clarity or a potential opportunity, take action and don't squander it. Learn from missed opportunities and commit to being more nimble in the future.

2. The perception of events as good or bad can change over time. The Taoist parable of the farmer highlights the idea that it's difficult to determine the ultimate outcome or value of an event. Crises and challenges may lead to unforeseen growth and success.

3. People can thrive and find happiness even after experiencing tragic events or setbacks. The story of Taylor Lindsay-Noel, a quadriplegic who turned her adversity into a successful business, demonstrates the power of reevaluating passions and rearchitecting life in the face of challenges.

4. Crisis can be an opportunity for personal growth and reinvention. Martha Stewart's example shows that even after facing criminal charges and serving time in prison, individuals can bounce back, embrace new opportunities, and continue to succeed.

5. Embrace uncertainty and be open to unexpected paths. Life is filled with twists and turns, and sometimes the most unexpected

situations can lead to personal and professional fulfillment.

Shifting Perspectives: Embracing Opportunities in Crises and Unexpected Paths

1. Embrace crisis as an opportunity: Crises can be catalysts for growth and transformation. Instead of succumbing to fear or despair, use crises as opportunities to reach new heights and explore new possibilities.

2. Face everything and work backward from the worst-case scenario: When confronted with a crisis, focus on surviving and finding practical solutions. By envisioning the worst-case scenario and planning accordingly, you can better navigate through challenges.

3. Listen to your instincts and act decisively: Trust your intuition and make bold decisions. Don't let fear or the need for approval hold you back. Take ownership of your choices and be willing to pivot when necessary.

4. Learn from missed opportunities and be nimble: If you miss an opportunity due to indecision, don't dwell on it. Instead, learn from the experience and commit to being more agile in the future. Be open to reversing course and seizing new opportunities.

5. Good and bad are subjective: Events that initially appear negative can lead to unexpected positive outcomes. Adopting a perspective of "good, bad, who's to say?"

allows you to see the potential in every situation and find growth even in adversity.

6. Leverage your past experiences: Draw strength from past hardships and use them as fuel for resilience. Your past struggles can provide valuable lessons and empower you to thrive in difficult situations.

7. Take action even without external pressure: Don't wait for a crisis to force you into action. Recognize that complacency can hinder progress. Chase the threat and actively pursue opportunities for growth, even in times of stability.

8. Embrace discomfort and uncertainty: Life is fluid and messy. Embrace the discomfort and uncertainty that come with it. Be patient and kind to yourself as you navigate the journey of personal and professional growth.

9. Make an impact and help others: Use your experiences and successes to make a difference in the world. Look for ways to contribute and uplift others, leveraging your unique strengths and abilities.

Thriving in Crisis: Embracing Growth, Trusting Instincts, and Seizing Opportunities

1. Embrace limitations and make decisive choices: Having too many options can paralyze us. Embrace the power of limitations and make decisive choices, even if it means letting go of other possibilities.

2. Don't be afraid of the dark side of options: Having too many options can lead to regret and indecision. Having fewer options can foster gratitude and commitment to the choices we make.

3. Crises provide opportunities for growth: Bad things will happen, but crises also offer opportunities to shine, prosper, and make significant progress. Embrace challenges and use them as catalysts for growth and new paths.

4. Run toward challenges instead of away from them: Instead of avoiding or being derailed by challenges, face them head-on. Approach crises as opportunities for value extraction and growth, finding ways to thrive even in difficult situations.

5. Continuously ask critical questions: Regularly ask yourself what the worst-case scenario would be and how you would handle starting from scratch. These questions help you

prepare for challenges and extract value from difficult situations.

6. Break patterns and unlock your true potential: Learn from past experiences, improve, and realize that what once seemed impossible can be achieved. Break free from limiting patterns and embrace the belief that you can overcome obstacles and achieve greatness.

Navigating External Obstacles: Retaining Control and Balancing Independence with Collaboration

1. Recognize external obstacles: Be aware of external patterns and circumstances that can hinder your progress. One common obstacle is partnering with the wrong person, especially when they are resistant to change or innovation. Assess whether you truly need a partner or if you could hire an employee with the necessary skills instead.

2. Retain control and evaluate needs: Maintain control of your business by carefully considering the areas where you lack expertise and creating a network of trusted individuals who can provide advice and support. You can bring in consultants or experts for specific problems without committing to long-term partnerships.

3. Balance solo and team dynamics: Solo founders have a higher survival rate for their businesses compared to teams, according to a study. However, businesses with multiple founders have a higher likelihood of becoming billion-dollar companies. Consider the benefits and drawbacks of working alone versus collaborating with others, ensuring that partnerships are born out of necessity rather than insecurity.

Building Successful Partnerships: Recognizing Warning Signs and Fostering Alignment

1. Tension: Subtle signs of friction during interactions with potential partners may indicate deeper conflicts within the partnership. If there is tension during the investor pitch, it is likely that the situation behind closed doors is even worse.

2. Divergent theories of change: Both partners should share a common vision and belief in the need for change within the industry. If one partner is resistant to doing something different or lacks conviction in the necessity of change, it can create a barrier to success.

3. Lack of differentiated roles: Each partner should have a distinct and well-defined role within the business. Overlapping areas of expertise or unclear ownership of responsibilities can lead to confusion and inefficiency.

4. Mismatched temperaments: Partners should present a unified front and avoid creating a dynamic where employees can exploit differences between them. Consistency and alignment in communication and decision-making are essential for stability and success.

5. Misalignment of effort: All partners must be fully committed and equally invested in the venture. If one partner is not putting in the

same level of effort as the others, it can lead to resentment and failure. Maximum commitment from all team members is necessary for sustainable success.

The Power of Investors: Influencing the Fate of Startups

Investors can have a significant impact on the success or failure of a startup.

When choosing investors, it is important to consider their potential negative influence and prioritize those who will not hinder progress.

The example of Juicero, a failed startup, highlights how investors can contribute to a company's downfall.

Juicero faced criticism for creating a seemingly unnecessary product after a video showed customers could squeeze the juice bags by hand.

Investors forced out Juicero's founder and CEO, which may have contributed to the company's failure.

Understanding a founder's vision, passion, and limitations is crucial when making investment decisions.

The right investors should support the founder's long-term goals and be aligned with their vision.

Stakeholders, including investors, can become obstacles if they don't provide support or align with the founder's vision.

It is important to minimize energy wasted on trying to please stakeholders who don't contribute positively to the company's success.

Giving power to stakeholders should be done judiciously, considering whether their involvement is truly necessary.

Navigating Investor Relationships: The Impact on Startup Success

Hesitant or demanding investors can hinder the progress of a startup, so it's important to choose investors who do not cause harm.

Juicero, a failed startup, faced criticism when customers discovered they could squeeze the juice bags themselves, making the expensive machine unnecessary.

Investors forced out Juicero's founder and CEO, which may have contributed to the company's downfall.

Understanding the strengths, limitations, vision, and passion of a founder is crucial when making investment decisions.

Juicero's founder saw the product as more than just a juicer and believed the investors didn't understand his long-term vision.

Stakeholders, including investors, can become obstacles if they don't support the founder's goals and vision.

Limited influence from investors may be challenging for companies that need outside funding.

Kozmo.com, a startup from the past, raised significant funding but ultimately failed due to a lack of profitability and a premature market.

Kozmo.com's CEO understood the future potential of e-commerce but realized that the market wasn't ready yet.

Building brand awareness and expanding quickly doesn't guarantee profitability.

Startups may need a substantial runway and financial resources to wait until the market is ready for their product or service.

Examples of other companies, such as Amazon and Tesla, facing financial challenges but surviving with sufficient funding.

Insufficient money to sustain the business can lead to its demise.

The readiness of the market and having enough financial runway are crucial factors for startup success.

Balancing Investor Relationships and Market Readiness: Lessons from Startup Failures and Successes

Timing of success is often unpredictable, and many people expect rewards too early.

Being early to an idea can be mistaken as being late because others may not share the same perspective.

Passing on an opportunity due to perceived competition in the market may lead to missed chances for success.

If you're unsure whether you're early or late, it's more likely that you're early and there is still significant potential for growth.

Boredom and impatience should not be the sole reasons to abandon an idea. Evaluate if there are valid reasons to exit.

Big bets in life need sufficient time to be proven right, and it's challenging to predict the exact timing of success.

Startup companies typically take at least three years to stabilize and around five years to see substantial returns.

Investment in RESY, a restaurant reservations service, faced timing uncertainties and had to adapt its business model.

RESY initially aimed to capture value by monetizing prime restaurant inventory but pivoted to become a superior back-end system for top restaurants.

The world wasn't ready for RESY's initial model, and fundraising efforts initially fell flat.

The company stabilized by iterating and eventually sold to American Express for a substantial amount.

The original value proposition of RESY still holds potential, but the market's readiness may be a determining factor.

Navigating Market Readiness and Avoiding Comparison Pitfalls

Kozmo faced challenges not only because the market wasn't ready for their model but also because they were compared to companies that were ahead of them in their journey, like Webvan.

The collapse of competitors in the same market can negatively impact the perception of other similar companies, hindering their investment opportunities.

Being early in a market requires being self-reliant and creating a unique story rather than being compared to lesser versions or competitors.

External obstacles such as partners, investors, money, and timing can be fatal, but internal patterns and personal behaviors are equally important to address.

CEOs often fall into the trap of trying to handle everything themselves, micromanaging employees, and getting bogged down in operations instead of focusing on scaling themselves up and leading with vision.

Successful leaders need to delegate, trust their team, and focus on strategic leadership rather than getting caught up in day-to-day operations.

The analogy of head coaches in football demonstrates the challenge of transitioning from a specialized role to a leadership position.

Letting go of micromanagement and empowering employees is essential for scaling and success.

Navigating Early Market Challenges and Transitioning to Strategic Leadership in Startups

Head coaches in the NFL often struggle to transition from being play callers to overseeing the entire team, which can lead to their firing within a few years.

Good leaders need to evolve and occupy the complete role of a head coach, which includes hiring talented individuals and not feeling threatened by their abilities.

In the business world, leaders need to fill endless roles and render themselves obsolete in most tasks to ensure the smooth functioning of the business.

Leaders should hire people who are better than them at specific tasks and celebrate their abilities rather than feeling resentful.

Micromanagement hinders employee satisfaction and productivity, and leaders should trust and appreciate their team members.

Scaling requires understanding one's strengths and weaknesses and recognizing where others can contribute effectively.

Strategic alliances and leveraging different strengths can benefit both individuals and organizations in various fields, whether in politics or business.

Leaders must be fearless in giving others the opportunity to shine and recognize when it's necessary to hire senior leaders to support the organization's growth.

Making the right hires in senior positions is crucial, as a bad hire can have catastrophic consequences.

One person alone cannot do it all, and hiring talented individuals is essential for the success and longevity of the company.

The Art of Leadership: Embracing Collaboration, Delegation, and Hiring the Right Talent

Going big and taking risks is crucial when you have a winner. Winners are rare, and playing small means losing out on potential gains.

Fear of being wrong and rational thinking can hinder the decision-making process, but following our hearts and trusting our instincts is important.

Instead of making small bets and splitting the difference, it's better to go all in on opportunities that are worth pursuing.

Investors who play small and make scattered investments are less likely to drive breakout success.

Leaders need to take risks and lead, rather than playing it safe and staying small.

In investment negotiations, the Sharks on The Vault insist on more equity because significant energy and time investment require a proportionate upside.

Every decision has an opportunity cost, and investing time in one venture means passing up other opportunities.

Finding winners often requires exploring numerous potential businesses or deals, but once winners are identified, it's important to hold on and commit.

Playing small limits the potential to achieve big dreams, and taking decisive action is necessary for significant success.

Investing Wisely: Navigating Hype, Avoiding Manipulation, and Making Informed Decisions

Following the herd and buying into hype can lead to poor investment decisions.

The example of Theranos, a fraudulent health tech company, demonstrates the dangers of being swayed by a compelling story and high-profile names associated with a company.

The board of directors at Theranos included notable figures who lacked relevant expertise in the industry, raising suspicions about the company's claims.

Emotional responses and the desire to avoid missing out can cloud judgment and make individuals susceptible to manipulation.

The availability cascade phenomenon contributes to the spread of fake news and the perception of credibility based on repeated exposure.

Shady entrepreneurs can leverage hype, media coverage, and influential endorsements to create an illusion of credibility and attract investors.

It's crucial to critically evaluate information, question manipulative tactics, and not be swayed by hype when making investment decisions.

Seeking independent verification, conducting thorough due diligence, and relying on reliable sources are essential in avoiding the trap of buying into false narratives.

Strategic Investing and Navigating Business Decisions: Lessons in Hype, Value, and Adaptability

Availability entrepreneurs understand and exploit the dynamic of spreading hype to promote their agenda and attract investors.

Betting on the greater fool theory may yield short-term gains, but it can lead to negative consequences and damage one's integrity in the long run.

It's important to stick with entrepreneurs who deliver real value rather than those who solely rely on persuasion and hype.

Letting go of a failing business or idea is difficult but necessary for growth and avoiding further losses.

The sunk cost fallacy, where the justification for continued investment is based on previous investments, should be avoided.

Signs of traction and response from the market are crucial indicators to determine the viability of a business.

Fundraising rounds and the increasing dilution of stakes can signal a point of no return and the need for reevaluation.

Asking hard questions about the business's purpose, opportunity cost, progress, and relevance in the current Sameeret is essential.

Winners have multiple ideas throughout their lifetime, and letting go of one idea opens up opportunities for new ones.

Making course corrections and embracing pivots is crucial for success, and successful individuals do so willingly and proactively.

Launching Success: Small Adjustments, Founder Fit, and the Power of Purpose

The pursuit of a major goal is comparable to launching a spacecraft, where big decisions and small adjustments are necessary for success.

Great leaders recognize the importance of small course corrections to stay on track and prevent disastrous outcomes.

Even if a business idea and its leader are great individually, it doesn't guarantee success if they are not the right match.

Founder/product fit, or alignment between the leader and the business, is crucial for long-term success and fulfillment.

It's important to follow one's true passion and calling, rather than pursuing something for the sake of capability or opportunity.

The presence of a deep, unexplainable drive and a sense of destiny can sustain leaders through the challenges and drudgery of building a business.

Supporting individuals who radiate a sense of inevitability and alignment with their dreams is preferable to backing someone who lacks that passion and purpose.

Pursuing a dream should feel like a calling that ignites a sense of purpose and dedication, even in the face of challenges and crises.

Navigating the Path to Success: Choosing Investors, Timing, and Staying True to Your Vision

1. Choose investors wisely: When seeking outside investment, be cautious of investors who may hinder your progress or not align with your vision. Look for investors who understand and support your goals and are willing to provide the necessary support throughout your journey.

2. Money alone is not enough: While funding is essential for business growth, it's important to recognize that success is not solely determined by the amount of money raised. Focus on building a sustainable business model and achieving milestones that demonstrate traction and value.

3. Timing is uncertain: Predicting the timeline of success is challenging, and being too early or too late can have significant implications. Trust your instincts and be willing to take calculated risks, even if others don't see the same opportunities.

4. Don't get caught in the hype: Beware of falling into the trap of following trends or investing in companies based solely on hype and popularity. Conduct thorough research, evaluate the underlying value and potential of the business, and avoid being swayed by manipulative tactics.

5. Letting go can be necessary: Recognize when
   it's time to let go of a business idea or venture
   that is not gaining traction or showing signs of
   success. Don't succumb to the sunk cost
   fallacy and continue investing resources into a
   failing endeavor. Be willing to pivot or
   explore new opportunities that align better
   with your goals and passions.

6. Be the right leader for your business: Ensure
   there is a strong alignment between your
   personal passion, expertise, and the business
   you're leading. If you lack genuine passion and
   commitment for the industry or idea, it may
   not be the right fit for you. Seek opportunities
   where you feel a sense of purpose and
   inevitability.

7. Develop leadership readiness: Leadership
   requires readiness, maturity, and the necessary
   skill set. Be honest with yourself about your
   readiness to take on a leadership role and
   invest in personal growth and development to
   acquire the skills and experience needed to
   effectively lead.

8. Execution is crucial: Ideas alone are not
   enough; successful execution is key. Focus on
   building and executing a solid business plan,
   developing proprietary aspects, and delivering
   value to customers. Execution separates
   winners from those who simply have ideas.

9. Be open to course corrections: Embrace the
   need for course corrections and be willing to
   make necessary adjustments along the way.

Stay adaptable, learn from failures, and iterate on your ideas and strategies to maximize your chances of success.

10. Trust your instincts: Ultimately, trust your instincts and follow your own path. Avoid being swayed by fear, external pressure, or the opinions of others. Stay true to your vision and pursue opportunities that align with your values and long-term goals.

Leadership Essentials: Confidence, Humility, and Self-Awareness

1. The strength of the founder matters: A great founder can overcome a weak idea, but a weak founder will struggle to succeed even with a great idea. The right blend of confidence and humility, along with self-awareness, is crucial for leadership success.

2. Confidence and humility: Successful leaders possess a balance of confidence and humility. They believe in their abilities, are unafraid to pivot when necessary, and can admit when they're wrong. They make decisions promptly when the need becomes evident.

3. The fish rots from the head: The leader sets the tone for the company. If the leader lacks the right qualities and mindset, it can hinder the company's success. Look for leaders who have the necessary qualities to lead and inspire others.

4. Iteration and self-awareness: Winners iterate and continuously improve their products or services based on feedback and data. Self-awareness allows leaders to recognize where things have gone wrong and make necessary adjustments. It also inspires trust and support from others.

5. Backing the right people: When evaluating investment opportunities, look for founders who are passionate, self-aware, and have the

determination to pursue their dreams. Supporting the right people at the right inflection point can lead to successful partnerships.

6. Recognizing the need for change: The case of immi, the ramen company, highlights the importance of recognizing when a product or idea needs improvement. The founders' self-awareness and their commitment to refining the product played a significant role in garnering support and achieving success.

7. Enlisting others to the cause: Successful leaders have a magnetic power to inspire and enroll others in their vision. Their self-awareness and ability to course correct when needed create a sense of trust and belief among supporters.

The Power of Self-Awareness and Open Dialogue: Key Takeaways

The opposite of self-awareness is ignorance or delusion. It's important to recognize that hiding or ignoring problems will only lead to their eventual revelation and potential negative consequences.

Having difficult conversations and getting everything out in the open, even if uncomfortable, is crucial for growth and understanding. Relying on assumptions can be inefficient and unreliable.

Bad leaders often try to avoid conversations and hide issues in their businesses. Good leaders, on the other hand, actively seek out flaws and opportunities for improvement.

Transparency, authenticity, and the willingness to admit when you don't know something are essential qualities for leaders. Avoiding the truth or being inauthentic can hinder collaboration and success.

Psychologists can provide valuable insights into a leader's mindset, strengths, weaknesses, and misconceptions. Evaluating leaders from a psychological perspective can be as important as assessing financials and business metrics.

Leadership Insights: Psychological Evaluations, Feedback, and Growth

The importance of psychological evaluations in assessing leaders before making major deals or promotions. These evaluations can provide valuable insights into a leader's mindset, strengths, weaknesses, and misconceptions.

Feedback is a gift, and good leaders embrace it. They have the willingness to adjust, change, and take feedback from others. They also possess emotional intelligence and the ability to deliver feedback effectively.

Strong performers are not afraid of causing conflict or expressing their opinions. They have the confidence to stand up for what they believe in, while still considering the perspectives of others.

Political savvy is crucial for success in the workplace. Leaders need to understand workplace dynamics, choose their words wisely, and adapt their approach to different individuals.

Valuing teamwork and acknowledging the contributions of others is important. Leaders who use "we" instead of "I" when discussing successes demonstrate their appreciation for the people around them.

Evading questions or being inauthentic can hinder leadership effectiveness. Leaders should be honest, authentic, and actively listen to others.

Recognizing weaknesses and having a willingness to grow and improve is key to personal and professional development.

Life is a continuous journey, and while achieving goals is satisfying, there is also joy in starting new ventures and looking ahead to the future.

Leadership Insights: Open Communication, Emotional Intelligence, and Continuous Growth

Problems and hidden truths cannot be hidden forever; it's essential to address them openly and get ahead of them before they become detrimental.

Hard conversations, though uncomfortable, are necessary for growth and success. Avoiding them can lead to inefficiency and misunderstandings.

Leaders who are transparent, authentic, and open are more trustworthy and effective. Hiding the truth or being inauthentic hinders progress and collaboration.

Investing in the assessment of a leader's psychological profile can provide valuable insights and help identify potential strengths and weaknesses.

Intellectual intelligence alone is not sufficient for success; emotional intelligence and the ability to work with others are equally important.

Having confidence and standing up for one's beliefs, while considering different perspectives, is crucial for effective leadership.

Developing political savvy and understanding workplace dynamics are essential for advancing in an organization.

Leaders who acknowledge and credit their team's contributions demonstrate the value they place on collaboration and teamwork.

Evading questions or lacking honesty and authenticity raises concerns and undermines trust.

Leveraging one's current advantages, relevance, and convening power can open doors to future opportunities.

Planning and taking action early on, even before transitioning from one phase to another, maximizes the potential for success.

Continuously seeking growth and embracing a perpetual growth mindset is key to ongoing success and achievement.

Strategies for Success: Leveraging Opportunities, Planning Ahead, and Building Skills

Leveraging status and relevance can open doors to valuable connections and opportunities.

Planning for the future and preparing for life beyond a current endeavor is crucial for long-term success.

Investing time and effort in internships or gaining experience outside of one's main field can provide valuable skills and insights.

Living within one's means and budgeting wisely, regardless of income level, can contribute to financial stability and growth.

A focused plan and attention to key evaluation criteria can help differentiate oneself and stand out in competitive environments.

Identifying and honing specific skills or strengths can give a competitive edge and enhance performance.

Being adaptable and finding alternative ways to prepare or overcome obstacles can lead to success even in challenging circumstances.

Unleashing the Power of Leverage: Identifying Assets and Embracing New Opportunities

Leveraging unique assets and qualities can open doors to opportunities and success.

Thinking creatively about how to utilize one's leverageable assets can lead to new possibilities and avenues for growth.

Recognizing and embracing the blurred lines between personal brand, influence, and business opportunities in today's world.

Everyone has a leverageable asset, whether it's a quality, circumstance, or personal story that can propel them towards their dreams.

Being untethered from fixed assumptions or systems can provide newfound freedom and the opportunity to explore new paths.

Reflecting on and identifying one's leverageable assets can help in determining the next steps and pursuing future success.

Unlocking Leverageable Assets: Building Success through Uniqueness and Strategic Planning

Identifying what you do better than anyone else and recognizing your unique skills or talents can be a leverageable asset.

Special access to certain people, networks, or knowledge can create opportunities for growth and success.

Your personal experiences and perspective on the world can provide valuable insights and empathy, shaping your approach and interactions with others.

Framing your challenges and struggles as opportunities for growth and understanding can be a leverageable asset.

Businesses also have leverageable assets that can be extended to create growth and success.

Leveraging previous experience and expertise can be applied to new ventures and industries.

Resourcing and strategic planning are crucial for revitalizing and scaling a business.

Leveraging name recognition and preserving the unique aspects of a brand can drive success and expansion.

Breaking Free from Conventional Progression: Taking Bold Leaps towards Success

Waiting for incremental progress or promotions can sometimes lead to stagnation and missed opportunities.

Taking big leaps and bypassing the traditional ladder can accelerate your path to success.

Misconceptions about what is necessary for success can hold you back. Challenging these misconceptions and taking bold actions can lead to significant progress.

Experience is important, but there is often an innate understanding of when you are ready to take the next step.

Be cautious of advice from individuals with compromised motives and consider the potential impact of their counsel on your growth trajectory.

Trust your own judgment and readiness, and don't let others dictate the pace of your progress.

Defying Conventional Wisdom: Embracing Bold Actions for Accelerated Success

Conventional wisdom often promotes incremental progress and following a predetermined sequence of events for success. However, this mindset can limit potential and delay progress.

Embracing a step change mindset and making big leaps can change the trajectory of your life and career.

Success is not always dependent on following a specific roadmap or paying dues. The greatest rewards often go to those who challenge the norm and refuse to conform to traditional expectations.

Decision-making based on passion and pursuing non-linear career paths can lead to faster learning and greater success.

Question the necessity of incremental steps and consider whether they truly contribute to your skills and growth or if they are driven by external expectations.

Avoid needless delays and embrace the inevitable by taking bold actions aligned with your aspirations and goals.

Breaking Free from Traditional Career Paths: Embracing Ambition and Challenging Limitations

Traditional corporate hierarchies often limit growth and career advancement, trapping individuals in incremental progress. It can be soul-crushing and hinder ambition.

Don't be afraid to quit a job if you feel you deserve more and see no path for growth within the organization. Moving to a new organization offers a fresh start and faster opportunities for advancement.

Avoid relying on one job to fulfill all career aspirations. If you're ambitious, you will likely outgrow the corporate world's pace of evolution.

Breaking away from the typical path can be challenging due to various factors, both within and outside of our control. It's important to acknowledge the weight and burdens that some individuals, particularly those from marginalized communities, carry in terms of representation and perception.

Recognize privilege and the advantages it may afford, such as not having to bear the weight of representing a race or gender.

Society should continue striving for progress on issues of race, gender, and representation to create a more equitable environment where everyone can make bold choices without undue burden or judgment.

Balancing Equity, Habituation, and Drive: Key Takeaways for Empowered Growth

The quest for equity and leveling the playing field should be a collective goal to ensure that everyone has agency and power over their destinies, irrespective of societal barriers and unfair advantages.

Exiting a job or taking risks can be intimidating at first, but with each experience, it becomes easier. Habituation plays a role in making certain actions more familiar and less daunting.

However, the downside of habituation is the potential loss of creativity and becoming robotic. It's essential to guard against becoming complacent and accepting limiting organizational structures and conditions.

Efficiency and increased performance can be gained through repetition and experience, enabling individuals to take on more simultaneously. However, it's important to strike a balance and avoid rushing to the next endeavor without fully maximizing the potential of the current pursuit.

Maintaining a drive and summoning the determination to reach new heights can be a challenge when confidence grows. It's crucial to stay focused and committed to each pursuit before moving on to the next.

From Commitment to Greatness: Nurturing Ideas, Embracing Challenges, and Sustained Achievement

It's important to stick with your ideas and see them through to execution instead of constantly chasing after someone else's ideas. Don't be a grasshopper that jumps from one idea to another without fully realizing the potential of your own.

By staying committed to your ideas and seeing them through, you give yourself the opportunity to reap the rewards of your insights and hard work. Leaving too soon may prevent you from capitalizing on the full potential and impact of what you've created.

The pursuit of greatness requires shifting motivational systems from the pressure-driven mindset to a mindset focused on reaching ever higher levels of potential. It's about giving your all and constantly pushing the boundaries of what you can achieve.

Maintaining self-esteem and avoiding a trail of unfinished projects requires committing to seeing ideas through and not succumbing to the temptation of constant novelty or external pressure.

By embracing the pursuit of greatness and continually challenging yourself, you create the conditions for sustained growth and achievement.

Unleashing Potential: Building on Achievements, Embracing Opportunities, and Cultivating Confidence

Continuously build on your successes and achievements to move closer to your desired future. Each accomplishment opens up new possibilities and positions you for the next milestone.

Embrace the thought experiment of ignoring limits and imagining what you would do if you believed you could do anything. This exercise can help uncover your true ambitions and aspirations.

Don't be afraid to explore new opportunities and say yes to things that may seem unexpected. Jesse Palmer's journey from backup quarterback to television host showcases the importance of being open to different paths and trying new things to discover your passions.

Take the first step towards your highest ambition. Start taking action, whether it's making a call, building a website, or prototyping a product. Use your past experiences, strengths, and courage to propel yourself forward.

Even celebrities face challenges and constraints in pursuing their entrepreneurial ventures. Scarlett Johansson's skincare brand, The Outset, emerged from her own personal struggle with acne and a desire to provide a simple and effective solution for others.

Confidence plays a crucial role in pursuing your dreams. As you gain confidence in your abilities and perspectives, you become more willing to share your unique point of view and make a positive impact.

Dreams Amplified: Partnerships, Resources, and Connections on the Path to Success

Recognize when you need to partner with others to bring your dream to fruition. Scarlett Johansson's collaboration with Kate Foster for The Outset exemplifies the importance of finding someone who shares your passion and has the expertise to turn your idea into a successful venture.

Consider the ingredients and resources you need to bridge the gap between where you are now and where you want to be. Consolidate the gains and knowledge from your previous experiences to increase your chances of success in your next endeavor.

Leaping alone is rare. Embrace the greatness of others and seek partnerships and collaborations that can amplify your efforts and bring diverse perspectives and skills to the table.

The encounter with Gary Vaynerchuk highlights the power of connecting with individuals who possess foresight and can identify emerging trends and shifts in the business landscape. Surrounding yourself with people who can provide valuable insights and challenge conventional thinking can be instrumental in shaping your own path to success.

The Power of Collaboration: Scarlett Johansson's Partnership for Success

Scarlett Johansson recognized that she couldn't pursue her skincare brand, The Outset, alone. She partnered with Kate Foster, an experienced entrepreneur in the beauty and fashion industry, to bring her vision to life. Collaboration and finding the right team members are essential for turning ideas into successful ventures.

When pursuing your dream, consider the necessary ingredients and steps required to bridge the gap between your current position and your desired outcome. Consolidate the gains and lessons from previous experiences to increase your chances of success in your next endeavor.

Partnering with others can be beneficial in achieving greatness. The example of Scarlett Johansson's partnership with Kate Foster highlights the value of working with individuals who complement your skills and share your passion.

The story of meeting Gary Vaynerchuk emphasizes the importance of recognizing greatness in others. Gary's insights and predictions about the future of the internet and social media were far-sighted and proved to be accurate. Being open to learning from others and embracing their expertise can be instrumental in your own journey.

Collaboration, Ingredients, and Recognizing Greatness: Pathways to Achieving Your Dreams

Empathy is a crucial characteristic for success. It involves understanding and connecting with others, recognizing their needs and perspectives, and using that understanding to solve problems effectively.

Defiance is about maintaining a strong conviction and vision for the future, even in the face of opposition or challenges. It means advocating for your ideas and not being swayed easily. Standing up for what you believe in is important for driving positive change.

Paying attention to detail is essential. While perfectionism can be counterproductive, getting the details right and consistently putting effort into all aspects of your work can make a significant difference. The way you handle small tasks reflects your competence and can impact your overall performance.

The concept of "finish" emphasizes the importance of giving maximum effort until the very end. It's about maintaining focus, discipline, and determination to achieve your goals and finish strong. Avoid complacency and strive to do your best work until the finish line is crossed.

- Kelsey was a true Visionary. She had a deep understanding of technology, a keen eye for identifying trends, and the ability to envision the potential applications of her ideas. She recognized the power of social media and saw an opportunity to harness its data for real-time sentiment analysis. Her ability to see the future implications of her technology set her apart and made her a perfect fit for the Visionary role.

- The Visionary is the person who sets the long-term direction and strategy for the organization. They are forward-thinking, innovative, and constantly scanning the landscape for emerging trends and opportunities. They have the ability to connect dots, make predictions, and inspire others with their vision.

- In Kelsey's case, her vision led to the creation of a groundbreaking technology platform that could revolutionize how businesses gather and analyze consumer sentiment. Her ability to see the potential impact of her ideas propelled her company forward and attracted investors like myself.

- Every successful organization needs a Visionary who can steer the ship and provide a clear sense of direction. They set the goals, define the vision, and inspire others to work towards a shared future. Without a strong Visionary, an organization can easily lose its way and miss out on valuable opportunities.

- So, if you have a strong ability to see the bigger picture, identify trends, and envision the future, embrace your role as a Visionary. And if you don't naturally fit into this domain, recognize its importance and seek out individuals who can fill this role in your organization. Remember, each domain plays a critical part in building a structurally sound and successful organization.

Navigating the Journey as a Visionary Entrepreneur

1. Balancing Vision and Pragmatism: As a visionary entrepreneur, it's essential to have a clear vision for your business while also recognizing and addressing potential risks and uncertainties.

2. De-risking for the Future: Understanding the need to de-risk your business, especially when relying on partnerships or external factors beyond your control, can help ensure long-term stability and success.

3. Making Tough Decisions: Entrepreneurship often requires making difficult choices. Being self-aware and pragmatic can lead to decisions like selling a company earlier than anticipated to secure a positive outcome for stakeholders and investors.

4. Confidence and Adaptability: Confidence in your vision, combined with the ability to adapt to changing circumstances and opportunities, is crucial for success as a visionary entrepreneur.

5. Backing the Jockey, not Just the Horse: Recognizing and supporting individuals with true visionary qualities can greatly impact the success of a venture. It's important to invest in people who have the ability to see the future, make strategic decisions, and navigate challenges.

6. Maximize Opportunities: Continually seeking ways to build upon successes and push boundaries is key to moving closer to your desired goals. Each achievement opens up new possibilities and positions you for further growth.

7. Embrace Empathy, Defiance, Attention to Detail, and Tenacity: These traits, along with empathy for others, the ability to stand your ground, a focus on details, and a relentless pursuit of excellence, contribute to entrepreneurial success.

8. Building a Strong Team: As a visionary entrepreneur, it's vital to recognize your own strengths and weaknesses and assemble a talented team that complements your skills, filling key domains like vision, execution, communication, and catalyzation.

9. Never Stop Learning: Successful entrepreneurs continually seek knowledge, stay ahead of emerging trends, and challenge themselves to grow. Embracing a learning mindset enables the pursuit of new opportunities and the ability to adapt to changing landscapes.

10. Finish Strong: Maintaining a strong work ethic and giving your best effort until the very end is essential. Resist the temptation to become complacent or lose momentum when approaching the finish line.

The Essential Role of the Catalyst in Entrepreneurship

1. Bridging Vision and Execution: The Catalyst serves as the bridge between the Visionary's big ideas and the practical steps needed to turn those ideas into reality. They bring together the right people, create actionable plans, and oversee day-to-day operations.

2. Organized Motivation: Catalysts are skilled at organizing and motivating teams. They identify talented individuals, inspire them, and keep them engaged and focused on achieving the shared vision.

3. Calm Passion and Emotional Regulation: A great Catalyst possesses a calm passion that can lower the temperature in challenging situations. They regulate their emotions effectively, remaining composed and focused, which fosters trust and confidence among team members and stakeholders.

4. Thriving in Complexity: Catalysts excel in managing complex environments, such as highly regulated industries. They navigate shifting landscapes, adapt to changes, and help their teams thrive in the face of challenges.

5. Data-Informed Decision Making: Catalysts utilize data to make informed decisions and provide clarity amidst uncertainty. They analyze information, evaluate risks, and

maintain a sense of control, which instills confidence in their leadership.

6. Building Trust and Collaboration: By demonstrating emotional control, understanding others' perspectives, and actively listening, Catalysts build trust and foster effective collaboration within their teams and with external partners.

7. Focus on Long-Term Goals: Catalysts keep their sights set on the long-term goals while managing day-to-day operations. They balance the immediate needs with the broader vision, ensuring the organization stays on track toward its ultimate objectives.

8. Complementary to the Visionary: A Catalyst complements the Visionary's strengths and helps translate their ideas into actionable plans. The partnership between the Visionary and Catalyst is vital for bringing dreams to fruition.

Importance of the Executor in Entrepreneurship

1. Focusing on Execution: Executors are individuals who excel at their specific roles and responsibilities within an organization. They are task-oriented and skilled at executing their assigned duties with precision and excellence.

2. Avoiding Vision Envy: Executors should embrace their expertise and resist the temptation to constantly toggle between visionary and catalyst roles. By staying focused on their area of expertise, they can contribute significantly to the organization's success.

3. Recognizing the Value of Execution: Visionaries and catalysts should acknowledge and appreciate the role of Executors within the organization. Recognizing their contributions and avoiding mission creep ensures a harmonious working environment and effective execution of tasks.

4. Finding Fulfillment in Supporting Visionaries: Special talents lie in the willingness to support and serve visionaries rather than resenting them. Embracing a support role can lead to deep connections, personal meaning, and career growth.

5. Leaning into Support Roles: If your strengths lie in supporting visionaries and executing

tasks, embrace and excel in those roles. It's essential to be honest with yourself about your strengths and weaknesses and find fulfillment in being a world-class Executor.

6. Embracing Support Opportunities: Take advantage of opportunities to work alongside creative leaders and contribute to bringing their visions to life. Serving as an Executor in support of a visionary can lead to personal growth, learning, and meaningful experiences.

7. Leveraging Personal Connections: Building relationships and leveraging personal connections can open doors to fulfilling support roles. Seizing opportunities aligned with your strengths and interests can lead to long-term success and a limitless career.

The Power of Communication in Entrepreneurship

1. Storytelling as a Critical Skill: Effective storytelling is essential for entrepreneurs to communicate the mission and vision of their organization to various stakeholders, including investors, employees, customers, and the media. It is not an add-on skill but a fundamental aspect of driving the success of a business.

2. The Importance of a Skilled Communicator: Having a skilled communicator, such as Tom Carroll, who can surface and articulate the company's story, is invaluable. Their expertise in storytelling can help shape the narrative and create a compelling brand image, resonating with both consumers and B2B audiences.

3. Emotional Connection in B2B Marketing: While storytelling is often associated with B2C marketing, it is equally important in B2B Sameereting. Behind every business decision-maker is an individual consumer who relies on emotional connections and beliefs when making purchasing decisions. Effective storytelling can establish those connections and drive successful B2B Sameereting.

4. Closing the Gap with Communication: Communication plays a critical role in bridging the gap between being ahead of the curve and gaining wider acceptance. By effectively distilling and disseminating the

organization's message, entrepreneurs can accelerate understanding and buy-in from the market.

5. Patience in the Face of Recognition: Entrepreneurs, like Cathie Wood, may face challenges in getting others to see their vision and recognize the potential of their ideas. It can take time for the Sameeretplace to catch up with visionary thinking, and entrepreneurs must exercise patience and persistence in advocating for their ideas.

6. The Power of Bold Calls: Making audacious calls and predictions, like Cathie Wood's $400 price target for Tesla, requires conviction and foresight. Even if initially met with skepticism, bold calls can pave the way for future recognition and market acceptance.

7. Evolving Communication for Success: As industries and consumer expectations change, entrepreneurs must adapt their communication strategies. Incorporating new tools and channels, such as social media and direct-to-consumer communication, can help businesses effectively convey their message and differentiate themselves in the market.

Building a Dream Team and Dealing with Difficult People

1. Core Competencies of a Great Organization: The four domains of a great organization are the Visionary, the Catalyst, the Executor, and the Communicator. Each domain plays a crucial role in driving the success of the organization, and individuals accountable for these domains need to excel in their respective areas.

2. The Importance of a Dream Team: Successful entrepreneurs understand the value of surrounding themselves with a dream team of talented individuals who complement their own skills and fill the necessary roles. Building a team of experts who can execute tasks, provide strategic guidance, and support the founder is essential for achieving goals.

3. The Role of a Skilled Communicator: A skilled Communicator is essential in translating the organization's vision into a compelling story that resonates with stakeholders. Effective storytelling and communication can bridge the gap between the vision and its execution, helping to garner support and understanding from various audiences.

4. Recognizing and Dealing with Difficult People: Difficult individuals within an organization, such as Withholders, Hijackers, Victims, Martyrs, and Vampires, can impede

progress and limit the potential for success.
Identifying and addressing toxic behavior is
crucial to maintaining a healthy and
productive work environment.

5. Leveraging Individual Strengths:
    Understanding one's own gifts and recognizing
    the strengths of team members is essential for
    harnessing the collective power of the
    organization. Each member should focus on
    their area of expertise and contribute their
    unique skills to drive success.

6. Importance of a Well-Structured Team:
    Having a team with diverse skill sets,
    including expertise in areas like investment
    management, legal counsel, and negotiation,
    can provide the necessary support for the
    entrepreneur to excel in their role. A well-
    structured team enables effective execution
    and decision-making.

Dealing with Difficult People

1. Avoid Difficult People: Whenever possible, it is advisable to avoid dealing with difficult people who exhibit rude, dismissive, hostile, or disrespectful behavior. Behaviors directed at others are likely to eventually be directed at you. Exceptions can be made for artists, considering the idiosyncrasies often associated with creative individuals.

2. Watch for Red Flags: When negotiating with others, particularly investors, partners, or employees, it's important to pay attention to their behavior and how they present themselves. If their best selves already display difficult or intolerable behavior, it's unlikely to improve over time. Recognize the red flags and act accordingly.

3. Five Toxic Patterns to Avoid: There are five common patterns of behavior that can bring individuals and organizations down. It is crucial to avoid embodying these patterns and to be cautious when interacting with individuals who exhibit them. These toxic personalities should be avoided to maintain a healthy and productive work environment.

4. Set Boundaries: Establishing clear boundaries and not tolerating meanness or cruelty is essential in dealing with difficult people. While some idiosyncrasies may be indulged for the right person, it is important to maintain

respect and ensure that toxic behavior is not encouraged or enabled.

5. Trust Your Instincts: If you sense that someone's behavior is toxic or detrimental to your well-being or the success of your organization, trust your instincts and take action. It is better to distance yourself from toxic individuals early on rather than hoping for improvement that may never come.

Dealing with Difficult People

1. Withholders: Withholders are individuals who struggle to deliver praise and feel threatened by others' success or skills. They are driven by insecurity or a need for dominance, resenting those who possess qualities they lack or who don't share their self-loathing. Withholders aim to bring others down instead of celebrating their achievements.

2. Beware of Dependency: If you rely heavily on mentorship or seek approval from someone who is a Withholder, you may find yourself trapped in a vicious cycle. Withholders exploit the assumption that hard work will be recognized and rewarded, causing distress and frustration for those around them.

3. Leave Toxic Environments: If you find yourself working for a Withholder, it is important to recognize that you cannot win in such a situation. Leaving the toxic environment becomes necessary to protect your well-being and professional growth. Withholders will continue taking advantage as long as you allow it.

4. Stop Withholding: If you suspect that you might exhibit Withholder tendencies, it is crucial to address this behavior. Learn to praise and appreciate the people around you, recognizing and maximizing their strengths. Opening your heart to gratitude and support

will lead to personal growth and improved relationships.

5. Unlock the Power of Support: Supporting those around you brings only positive outcomes. By fostering a culture of recognition and encouragement, you create an environment where individuals can thrive and reach their full potential.

Dealing with Hijackers

1. Hijackers: Hijackers are individuals who not
    only withhold praise but also exhibit
    aggressive behavior. They seek to take
    advantage of others' talents and achievements,
    exploiting vulnerabilities for their own gain.
    They may attempt to claim credit for someone
    else's work or undermine their success.

2. Empathy and Fairness: To extract genuine
    value from creative genius, it is essential to
    approach interactions with empathy and
    fairness. Instead of exploiting the deficiencies
    of others, great leaders recognize and support
    their strengths. They pay fair wages and
    advocate for the well-being of their workforce,
    even when individuals may lack the courage to
    ask for what they deserve.

3. Supporting Vulnerable Individuals: A leader's
    responsibility includes compensating and
    supporting individuals who may be less
    inclined or able to assert themselves. By
    providing a secure environment, leaders
    enable individuals to unleash their full
    potential and contribute their unique gifts.

4. Building Confidence: Encouraging individuals
    to stand up for themselves and demand fair
    treatment is crucial. Leaders can play a role in
    helping vulnerable individuals develop
    confidence and overcome their fear of
    confrontation. This empowers them to protect

their work, assert their value, and establish healthy boundaries.

5. Success Stories: Sharing success stories of individuals who have overcome Hijackers can inspire others and serve as a reminder that their work has value. By highlighting the journey of individuals who have gained confidence and achieved success, leaders can encourage others to persevere and advocate for themselves.

Avoiding the Victim Mentality

1. The Victim Mentality: Victims are individuals who constantly perceive injustice and believe that they are unfairly targeted. They build their identity around their negative experiences and setbacks, viewing every obstacle as confirmation of their victimhood. This mindset hinders personal growth and success.

2. Gratitude and Resilience: Good performers approach life with gratitude and resilience. They don't feel entitled to success but instead appreciate and celebrate their achievements when they occur. They view setbacks as opportunities for learning and growth, rather than as evidence of victimization.

3. Shifting Perspectives: During challenging times, it's important to shift perspective and ask, "Why not me?" This mindset acknowledges that everyone faces difficulties and believes in one's ability to handle and overcome them. Embracing a sense of resilience and resourcefulness can empower individuals to face adversity head-on.

4. Finding Strength in Differences: Embracing one's unique circumstances, scars, or challenges can foster a sense of exceptionalism and pride. Instead of lamenting their situation, individuals can find strength and resilience in their differences, recognizing that they are not defined by their circumstances but by their response to them.

5. Crisis Amplifies Strengths and Weaknesses: A crisis has a way of amplifying an individual's existing traits and attitudes. Victims may find their victimhood magnified during challenging times. It's crucial to avoid falling into the victim trap and instead focus on building resilience, optimism, and determination.

6. Last Word Until the Last Breath: Embracing the belief that one always has the ability to choose their response and mindset, individuals can overcome victimhood. By taking ownership of their lives and refusing to succumb to a victim mentality, individuals retain control and agency over their actions and outcomes.

Breaking Free from Martyrdom

1. Martyr Mentality: Martyrs are individuals who take on excessive workloads and burdens, spreading themselves too thin and sacrificing their own well-being. They do so not out of genuine altruism or team support, but to confirm their narrative of being unjustly burdened. They often struggle to perform optimally and drain the organization psychologically.

2. Coachable Nature: Martyrs are receptive to coaching and can be guided towards healthier behaviors. By helping them understand that delegating tasks to individuals best suited for them is a greater service to the cause, they can redirect their energy towards empowering others instead of carrying the entire load themselves.

3. Transitioning from Martyr to Leader: CEOs may fall into the trap of martyrdom, especially if they lack experience, maturity, or fear conflict. When bootstrapping a company, it can be challenging to shift gears and delegate responsibilities once resources become available. CEOs must evolve their definition of their role and recognize the importance of effective delegation.

4. The Illusion of Accomplishment: Bad leaders often reward martyrs for their hard work, failing to distinguish between mere activity and actual accomplishment. Martyrdom and

victimhood are two sides of the same coin, with both mentalities absolving individuals of agency and assigning blame to external factors. Recognizing this pattern is crucial for personal and organizational growth.

5. Taking Agency and Responsibility: Breaking free from martyrdom requires individuals to take ownership of their destiny and reject the notion that the universe or external circumstances dictate their success or failure. By embracing agency, individuals can redirect their energy towards productive actions and collaborate with others to achieve meaningful outcomes.

6. Cultivating Effective Leadership: Effective leaders recognize the value of balance, delegation, and optimizing team performance. They understand that martyrdom hinders long-term success and seek to create a culture where individuals feel empowered, supported, and able to contribute their best work.

Recognizing and Confronting Corporate Vampires

1. Identifying Corporate Vampires: Vampires in the corporate world manipulate and distort reality, often exhibiting narcissistic traits. They combine the negative qualities of Withholders, Hijackers, Victims, and Martyrs, attempting to convince others that their perception is inaccurate and dismissing valid concerns or criticisms.

2. Elizabeth Holmes and Theranos: Elizabeth Holmes, the founder of Theranos, exemplifies a corporate Gaslighter. She deflects blame and denies wrongdoing, insisting that others are misinterpreting the situation. Eventually, her deception was exposed, much like the collapse of Enron under CEO Jeffrey Skilling's manipulation tactics.

3. Gaslighting's Detrimental Effects: Vampires undermine trust, create a toxic work environment, and impede organizational progress. Their distortion of reality can lead to misaligned priorities, poor decision-making, and a culture of fear and uncertainty.

4. Challenging Vampires: Confronting corporate Vampires requires courage and persistence. It often requires individuals to trust their own perceptions and seek objective evidence to counter the manipulative narratives. Solidarity among employees and support from ethical

leaders are crucial in countering gaslighting behaviors.

5. Promoting Accountability and Transparency: Establishing a culture of accountability and transparency is vital in mitigating the influence of Vampires. Organizations should encourage open communication, foster trust, and provide channels for reporting and addressing manipulative behaviors.

6. Building Resilience and Empowering Individuals: Developing resilience in individuals can help them recognize and resist gaslighting tactics. Empowering employees through training, education, and fostering a supportive environment enables them to stand up against gaslighting and contribute to a healthier workplace culture.

7. Leadership's Role: Ethical leaders play a crucial role in combating gaslighting behaviors. They set a positive example, encourage open dialogue, and hold individuals accountable for their actions. By promoting a culture of honesty, integrity, and respect, leaders can help prevent gaslighting tactics from taking hold.

The Power of Surrounding Yourself with Brilliance

1. Elevating Leadership through Brilliant Teams: Great leaders rise to new heights by surrounding themselves with individuals who excel in every aspect of the organizational puzzle. Empowering these talented individuals to maximize their potential leads to collective success and growth.

2. Talent-spotting and Enabling: Leaders have the opportunity to be talent-spotters, identifying individuals who are meant to excel in their respective capacities. By enabling and supporting them, leaders foster an environment where everyone can shine.

3. Selflessness and Self-Interest: Supporting others in their success can be both selfless and self-interested. Leaders can genuinely celebrate the achievements of those they support while also reaping the rewards of their contributions. Having a stake in their success ensures a tangible return for the efforts invested.

4. Phenomenal People at Every Level: The presence of exceptional individuals at all levels of an organization is a key indicator of success. Even if the founders themselves are not extraordinary, surrounding them with brilliant talent unleashes the full potential of the organization.

5. A-Player Hiring Strategy: The adage that "B players hire C players" to elevate their own standing can be transcended by hiring A players. When B players hire A players, they themselves are elevated to A-player status. Embracing and embracing brilliance does not diminish one's own shine.

6. Embracing Collaboration and Growth: Rather than solely focusing on competing for market share, a more effective growth strategy is to expand the overall market. Collaboration and the success of others in the same industry contribute to the growth and demand for exceptional products or services.

7. Brilliance is Not Zero-Sum: The success of others does not detract from one's own achievements. Embracing the idea that brilliance is not zero-sum creates a supportive ecosystem where multiple individuals and businesses can thrive simultaneously.

Unlocking Hidden Genius: Aidan Kehoe's Journey to Success

1. Seizing Opportunities: Aidan Kehoe's story exemplifies the power of recognizing and seizing opportunities, even in challenging circumstances. Starting as a restaurant dishwasher, he leveraged his skills, including storytelling, to progress in his career.

2. Entrepreneurial Drive: Aidan's entrepreneurial spirit led him to identify an unmet need in the cybersecurity industry. Recognizing the increasing threats faced by small and midsize businesses, he launched SKOUT CyberSecurity, positioning himself as a trusted expert in the field.

3. Hidden Genius: Aidan possessed inherent talents and a unique perspective, but lacked the skills to scale his business. Recognizing his potential, the author saw an opportunity to unlock Aidan's hidden genius and maximize his impact.

4. The Power of Coaching: Dr. Laura Finfer was brought in to help Aidan unlock his full potential. Through an honest assessment of the company and Aidan's leadership, she identified areas of improvement and presented a brutally honest report.

5. Embracing Vulnerability: Aidan's response to the report was remarkable. Rather than avoiding or dismissing the feedback, he

openly acknowledged his weaknesses and vulnerabilities. By sharing the report with his senior leadership team, he demonstrated transparency and a commitment to growth.

6. Creating a Culture of Imperfection: Aidan's bold move of sharing his weaknesses with his team created a culture where imperfections were acknowledged and embraced. This act of vulnerability fostered a sense of unity, highlighting that growth and improvement were a collective effort.

7. The Journey of Personal and Organizational Growth: Aidan's journey showcases the importance of self-awareness, continuous learning, and the willingness to address weaknesses. By embracing personal growth, he positioned himself and his organization for success.

The Challenging Journey of Transformation

1. Embracing Feedback: Aidan Kehoe's reaction to the honest and accurate feedback in Dr. Finfer's report was transformative. He recognized the value of the feedback as a roadmap for personal and professional growth, and committed to addressing each challenge presented.

2. Burning the Boats: Sharing the report with his team was a bold move for Aidan. By exposing his weaknesses and vulnerabilities, he demonstrated his commitment to improvement and showed his team how much he cared. This act of transparency created a foundation of trust and fostered a culture of self-awareness within the company.

3. Recognizing Imperfection: Aidan understood that hiding imperfections was futile because others already knew about them. By openly acknowledging his own flaws and committing to improve, he encouraged others in the company to have similar conversations about their own growth areas.

4. The Difficult Journey: Aidan's journey towards transformation was not without challenges. He faced personal challenges at home, including his son's autism diagnosis and his daughter's health issues. Additionally, the pressure from new investors who were

scrutinizing his performance added to the difficulty.

5. Navigating Investor Expectations: Aidan had to navigate the expectations of the new investors who were holding him to high standards. He realized the need to assemble a team that could communicate effectively with investors while also connecting on a human level with customers.

6. Balancing Soft and Technical Skills: Aidan recognized the importance of having an ambidextrous team that could speak the language of investors (Excel, numbers) while also connecting with customers on a human level. This balance was crucial in meeting the expectations of both investors and customers.

A Journey of Resilience and Triumph

1. Reaching a Breaking Point: Aidan's lowest moment came when personal challenges and pressure from new investors overwhelmed him. He felt like he was failing and contemplated leaving the business. The emotional toll and lack of sleep took a toll on him.

2. Support and Encouragement: Aidan reached out to Matt for support, expressing his feelings of inadequacy and desire to quit. Matt recognized Aidan's potential and refused to let him give up. He assured Aidan that he was not done and encouraged him to take a break to prioritize his family and well-being.

3. Surrendering and Rebuilding: Aidan experienced a release after surrendering to the situation. He embraced the support and took the necessary steps to rebuild the company and his own life. Over the next six months, he rebuilt his executive team, restructured the business model, improved communication, and focused on his personal health.

4. The Transformation: Aidan's relentless efforts and the collective team effort paid off. Two years after hitting rock bottom, SKOUT CyberSecurity was acquired by Barracuda Networks for a significant amount. Aidan's turnaround was a remarkable business accomplishment and a testament to his resilience.

5. Supportive Leadership: Aidan's journey was supported by Dr. Finfer, who provided guidance and coaching. Matt and the entire team rallied behind him, recognizing his intelligence, self-awareness, and motivation. The collaboration and collective effort played a vital role in turning the company around.

6. A Lasting Impact: Aidan's success not only resulted in financial rewards but also transformed the lives of those involved. The team's dedication and belief in Aidan's potential led to a remarkable business accomplishment that will have a lasting impact.

From Baseball Legend to Funeral Home Operator

1. Idolizing a Baseball Legend: Growing up, the author had a deep admiration for Andre Dawson, a renowned baseball player known as "The Hawk." Dawson's exceptional skills as a hitter and fielder, along with numerous accolades and induction into the Baseball Hall of Fame, left a lasting impression on the author.

2. A Surprising Career Transition: In 2003, long after his retirement from baseball, Andre Dawson embarked on an unexpected professional journey. He took on the role of running a funeral home in Miami, Florida, a stark contrast to his baseball career. This unique transition garnered attention from media outlets such as ESPN.

3. Embracing the Unforeseen Path: Despite the unconventional nature of his new profession, Dawson embraced the responsibilities of the funeral home. He approached each task, whether driving a hearse or greeting mourners, with dedication and a sense of purpose. Dawson acknowledged that he could never have predicted this path for himself but believed it might be his true calling.

4. Finding Fulfillment and Purpose: Dawson's involvement in the funeral home industry demonstrated his willingness to follow where life led him. Despite the stark contrast to his

baseball career, he found meaning in helping others during their most vulnerable moments. This unexpected calling allowed him to contribute to the community in a different, yet deeply meaningful, way.

From Baseball Player to Acclaimed Artist and Inspirational Figure

1. The Baseball Journey: Micah Johnson followed a path similar to that of Andre Dawson, climbing the ranks of professional baseball. He made his major league debut as the second baseman for the Chicago White Sox in 2015 but faced ups and downs in his career, playing for multiple organizations and spending time in the minor leagues.

2. Discovering a Passion for Art: While pursuing his baseball career, Johnson discovered a hidden passion for art. He started painting whenever he found the time, receiving affirmation and support from his teammates, which gave him the confidence to pursue art more seriously.

3. Transitioning to Full-Time Artistry: After retiring from baseball at the age of twenty-eight, Johnson made the bold decision to focus his energy and talent on his art. Recognizing the results of hard work and dedication from his baseball career, he applied the same principles to his art, committed to continuous improvement.

4. NFTs and Inspiring Children: In 2019, Johnson ventured into the world of NFTs (Non-Fungible Tokens) and embraced a new artistic mission. Prompted by a question from his young nephew about Black astronauts, Johnson embarked on creating art to inspire

children to dream big, regardless of their circumstances. He fully committed himself to this endeavor, relocating to New Hampshire with his family and generating significant sales through his art.

5. Achieving Astonishing Success: Johnson's dedication and artistic talent propelled him to remarkable success. He has generated over $2 million in sales, primarily revolving around his Black astronaut character, Aku. Aku has even become the first NFT property optioned by a television studio, amplifying the reach of Johnson's inspiring message.

6. Embracing the Nadir of Destiny: Johnson's journey serves as a testament to the idea that one's career peak may not be the ultimate destination. By embracing his passion for art and focusing on inspiring others, he has achieved astonishing success and found fulfillment in his second act as an artist.

Media Entrepreneur and Metaverse Pioneer

1. A Passion for Tech and Humanity: Laurie Segall's career as a journalist at CNN began in 2008, covering tech companies like Facebook and Apple. She was drawn to the world of tech and fascinated by the intersection of technology, humanity, and society.

2. Self-Starter Mentality: Segall's self-starter mentality drove her to create her own beat at CNN, covering the startup scene and launching the network's first streaming show. She craved being in control and moving fast, realizing she didn't want to wait for permission to pursue her ambitions.

3. Embracing Discomfort and Cutting the Cord: Inspired by a video about lobsters shedding their shells, Segall recognized that she needed to undergo a period of discomfort and shed her own professional shell. She made the decision to leave CNN and create her own media company, Dot Dot Dot, to tell stories on her own terms.

4. The Leap of Faith: Launching Dot Dot Dot was not without fear. Segall acknowledges that failure and the roller coaster of ups and downs are part of every journey. Despite loving journalism and being great at it, she knew it wasn't enough for her. She embraced the courage to face her fears and venture into the unknown.

5. Pivoting to the Metaverse: As her journey progressed, Segall realized that her future involved more than storytelling and content creation. She is pivoting Dot Dot Dot into a cross-platform media property that will bring the metaverse, Web 3.0, NFTs, and the future of the Internet to the masses. Leveraging her deep relationships in the tech space, Segall aims to connect users to the new online world and help them navigate its vast opportunities.

6. The Rewards of Independence: Leaving CNN and venturing out on her own gave Segall the independence to create her own vision and pursue her ideas without seeking approval from others. Despite not having prior business knowledge, she reached out for guidance and acknowledged the accomplishments of other remarkable women who have created successful businesses. The journey has been challenging yet rewarding, providing Segall with a newfound sense of fulfillment and privilege.

Finding Your Unique Path to an Impactful Life

1. Embrace Being Yourself: The key to a fulfilling life and career is finding a path that allows you to fully express yourself and unleash your power. Let go of self-censorship and fear of shining too bright. When you have the freedom to be your authentic self, you can achieve greatness and pursue your dreams with full commitment.

2. Going All In: Going all in on your dreams means not holding back and putting your whole self into your endeavors. Eliminate backup plans and hedges, and invest your mental energy into pursuing your passions without restraint. The journey may not always be smooth, but the rewards are worth it.

3. Different Journeys, Different Choices: Each person's journey is unique, and the decisions they make along the way depend on their values, circumstances, and aspirations. For example, entrepreneurs Courtney Claghorn and Sam Offit faced a choice between cashing out or continuing to grow their business. There is no right or wrong decision; it depends on individual priorities and desired lifestyle.

4. Freedom and Relief: The ultimate dream for many entrepreneurs is achieving financial freedom and relieving the pressure of their business. Selling a majority stake in their company allowed Courtney and Sam to

experience this freedom, think more clearly about life and business, and explore new opportunities such as charity work and supporting other startups.

5. Discovering Your Unique Path: Your journey will be different from others', driven by your own gifts, passions, and callings. Reflect on what you can uniquely offer based on your life experiences. Consider how you want to spend your days and the legacy you want to leave behind. The key is to find your path and follow it to lead an impactful life.

Embracing the Perpetual Pursuit: Finding Joy and Purpose Beyond Achievements

1. The Anticipation-Accomplishment Disparity: There's often a sense of letdown or melancholy after achieving a long-awaited goal, such as completing a marathon or closing a significant deal at work. The anticipation of the accomplishment tends to outweigh the actual experience. Research shows that how we feel during the activity matters more than our expectations beforehand or our memories afterward.

2. Olympians and the Pursuit of Happiness: Even Olympians experience psychological depletion and depression upon returning home from the games, particularly if they lack a plan for what comes next. Success and contentment are not finite destinations but are built upon perpetual pursuit. Ongoing growth and new challenges are essential for engagement and fulfillment.

3. The Discomfort of Success: High achievers may reach a point where being great at something is no longer enough. Michael Jordan retired at the peak of his basketball career, and Jon Stewart left The Daily Show because they recognized the need for discomfort and continued growth. Big achievements can lead to a sense of letdown, emphasizing the importance of progress and looking ahead to new possibilities.

4. Redefining Milestones: HBS professor
    Francesca Gino shares her experience with
    tenure and the potential emotional impact it
    can have. Instead of viewing tenure as a
    destination, she reframed it as a milestone in
    her larger journey of making a positive impact
    on the world. It's crucial to avoid seeing
    milestones as the ultimate goal but rather as
    stepping stones to further growth and
    achievement.

5. Embrace the Journey: While it's essential to
    acknowledge and be proud of your
    accomplishments, it's equally important to
    maintain a forward-looking perspective.
    Reflect on how far you've come, but always
    focus on how much further you can go. Find
    joy and purpose in the continuous pursuit of
    personal and professional growth.

The Rewards of Struggle: Embracing the Game of Life

1. Minimalism and the Pursuit of Satisfaction: Joshua Becker's philosophy of minimalism emphasizes the idea that possessions and accomplishments don't bring the fulfillment we expect. By decluttering our lives and focusing on what truly matters, we can find greater satisfaction and joy.

2. The Emptiness of Victory: Becker highlights the sense of emptiness felt in victory. When a goal is achieved, there may be a momentary high, but soon the pursuit of new goals begins. Winning doesn't change our lives in any significant way; it's the ongoing work and purpose that bring true fulfillment.

3. The Perpetual Pursuit of Happiness: Some people question the idea of constantly striving for new achievements and suggest that a life of leisure and basking in past glory would be more satisfying. However, the true joy lies in the struggle, pursuit, and purpose. Embracing challenges and pushing ourselves to grow is what keeps us truly happy.

4. Examples of Embracing the Game: Marc Lore, Bobbi Brown, and Gary Vaynerchuk are individuals who embody the philosophy of embracing the game of life. They could have rested on their laurels after achieving success but chose to continue pursuing new endeavors,

driven by their passion, the process, and the love of the game itself.

5. Gratitude for the Journey: Gary Vaynerchuk expresses his gratitude for the opportunity to play the game of business every day. He values the process, learns from losses, and remains motivated for future endeavors. Success and material possessions take a backseat to the deep satisfaction derived from being fully engaged in the game.

Embracing Disruption

1. Embrace Disruption: John Skipper's experience running a multibillion-dollar media company and later launching Meadowlark Media showed him the value of embracing disruption and seeing industries from a different perspective.

2. Freedom to Work on Meaningful Projects: Starting his own studio allowed John to work on projects that he valued and found personally rewarding. It gave him the freedom to choose the type of work and collaborate with people he admired.

3. Size Doesn't Define Success: John's transition from leading a major corporation to running a smaller venture taught him that success isn't solely determined by revenue or the size of the opportunity. Doing interesting and fulfilling work can be more rewarding than pursuing constant upward growth.

4. Authenticity and Values Matter: By having his own business, John could prioritize working with people who were not only talented but also genuinely humane and decent. This emphasis on values and creativity made the work more enjoyable and fulfilling.

5. Continuous Learning and Growth: Launching Meadowlark Media at a later stage in his career allowed John to learn new skills and experience the journey of starting a business

for the first time. It reminded him of the importance of always seeking new knowledge and personal growth.

Unleashing the Power of Busy

1. Don't Fall into the "Too Busy" Trap: Recognize the tendency to delay pursuing your passions and goals due to busyness, and break free from the status quo.

2. Leverage Today for Tomorrow: Embrace the idea of leveraging your current activities and projects to propel you towards your desired future, even if it means juggling multiple endeavors simultaneously.

3. The Right Time is Now: Waiting for the perfect moment will only hinder progress. Seize opportunities and launch new ventures during busy and exciting times when you have momentum and engagement.

4. Create Leverage, Don't Chase It: Leverage is most effective when you have a strong foundation and are proactive, rather than desperately seeking it when you're already in need.

5. Embrace Openness to Opportunity: Stay open to unexpected opportunities, even if the timing seems wrong. Trust that taking the first steps towards your ambitions will attract further support and serendipity.

6. A Life of Purposeful Busyness: Embrace a mindset of perpetual growth and activity, like Stephen Ross, who finds joy in being busy and continuously pursuing new ventures.

7. Save Space for Grace: Allow room for
    unexpected connections, ideas, and moments
    of serendipity that can shape and enhance your
    journey.

Embracing the Present and Seizing Opportunities

1. Don't Wait for the Perfect Time: The world will never align perfectly with your plans, so leverage what you're doing today to move closer to your goals.

2. Embrace Being Busy: Being busy doesn't have to hinder your progress. Use your momentum and leverage your current engagements to pitch new ideas and ventures.

3. Leverage Moments of Success: Seize fleeting moments of success and launch new ventures before you actually need to. Don't wait until desperation sets in to create opportunities.

4. Stay Open to Opportunity: Be open to unexpected opportunities, even if the timing seems wrong. Save space for serendipity and trust that the universe will support your efforts.

5. Embody the "Busy for Life" Mindset: Emulate the mindset of being engaged and active in pursuing your ambitions, as exemplified by individuals like Stephen Ross.

6. Enjoy the Journey: Embrace a perpetual growth mindset and find joy in the pursuit of your ambitions, appreciating every minute of the journey.

From Adversity to Empathy

1. Find Purpose in Adversity: Curtis Martin's difficult childhood experiences motivated him to find meaning and purpose in his life. He discovered that football could be a platform to help others and bring positive change.

2. Football as a Vehicle for Good: Martin saw football as a means to make a difference. He used his platform to connect with the homeless, offer support, and create safe spaces for influential individuals to share their struggles.

3. Empathy and Compassion: Despite the hardships he faced, Martin developed a remarkable sense of empathy, giving him the ability to connect with others on a deep level. He became an example of using personal experiences to uplift and inspire others.

4. Leveraging Talents to Help Others: Martin's story emphasizes the importance of using our unique abilities and talents to make a positive impact on people's lives, even in the face of adversity.

5. Transforming Pain into Wisdom: Instead of allowing bitterness or anger to consume him, Martin channeled his challenging experiences into developing wisdom, empathy, and a desire to help those who are less fortunate.

6. Inspiring Others: Curtis Martin's journey serves as an inspiration to find ways to use our strengths and passions to create positive change, even in the most challenging circumstances.

From Powerlessness to Empowerment

1. Personal Empowerment: The author's own experiences of feeling powerless and longing for a better life drive their commitment to making a difference in the lives of others. They see helping others as the ultimate goal and find fulfillment in being able to provide the support they never received.

2. Honoring a Mother's Legacy: Through the Linda J. Higgins Empowerment Scholarship, the author honors their mother's memory and empowers single mothers by providing them with opportunities for education. The scholarship recipients overcome incredible odds and inspire others with their resilience and determination.

3. Transformative Commencement Address: In the author's commencement address, they highlight the stories of scholarship recipients and acknowledge their strength and perseverance. They use their own childhood memories and the scholarship winners' experiences to emphasize the importance of not making excuses, overcoming victimhood, and never giving up.

4. Going Beyond Financial Support: The author strives to contribute more than just financial assistance to the scholarship recipients. They actively engage with the recipients, offer support beyond the monetary aspect, and

provide mentorship to help them navigate their journeys.

5. Stories of Triumph: The stories of scholarship recipients, such as a single mother bringing her daughter to class and a survivor of domestic violence battling cancer, showcase the incredible resilience and determination of these women. Their journeys inspire others and demonstrate the transformative power of education and support.

6. Rewriting a Legacy: By supporting these strong and defiant women through the scholarships, the author feels like they are rewriting their mother's story and ensuring that her legacy lives on. They find solace in knowing that their mother's memory is honored through the achievements and empowerment of the scholarship recipients.

7. Becoming a Messenger: The author sees themselves as a messenger for their mother's legacy, actively working to change lives and empower others. Through their actions and support, they aim to rewrite the ending of their mother's story and create a lasting impact.

Igniting Change: The Power of Individual Action

1. Learning from Failure: The author reflects on their first major failure as a student running for president of Queens College. Despite losing, they highlight the subsequent success and impactful careers of their opponents, José Peralta and Alan van Capelle. This experience emphasizes the importance of resilience and the potential for personal growth and transformative journeys even in the face of defeat.

2. Taking Action for Change: Alan van Capelle's commitment to advocating for marriage equality serves as an example of how individuals can make a difference by actively engaging in causes they believe in. He demonstrates that change starts with personal conviction and the willingness to challenge the status quo.

3. Fighting for Hearts and Minds: Alan's efforts to change public opinion and influence politicians highlight the multifaceted approach needed to create meaningful change. By engaging in advocacy work and addressing both societal attitudes and political structures, he played a pivotal role in the passage of marriage equality legislation.

4. The Ripple Effect: The success of Alan's advocacy work and José Peralta's election to the State Senate showcases the potential

impact of individual actions. By supporting and campaigning for José, Alan played a part in securing a crucial vote for marriage equality, demonstrating the power of collaborative efforts and the importance of leveraging opportunities for progress.

5. Empowering Others: The author encourages readers to recognize their own power to effect change. They emphasize that everyone has the ability to pick a cause that resonates with them and take steps to address systemic issues. By identifying points of maximum impact and actively working towards positive change, individuals can contribute to shaping a better future.

6. Moving the World in the Right Direction: The author urges individuals not to remain passive in the face of social issues that require attention and action. They highlight the need to open our eyes to injustices and situations that may be deemed acceptable today but could be regretted tomorrow. By recognizing the urgency and embracing their capacity for change, individuals can work towards creating a more just and equitable society.

From Dancing Star to Movement Leader

1. Recognizing Superpower: Julianne Hough's passion and talent for dance led her to realize its transformative power and its ability to change one's state of mind. She identified dance as her superpower and believed that it could be harnessed to bring joy, wellness, and empowerment to people around the world.

2. Creating a Holistic Experience: Julianne aimed to bring the immersive experience of shows like Dancing with the Stars to a broader audience. She envisioned a wellness platform, KINRGY, that combines dance-driven workouts with movement, strength work, breath work, visualization, and meditation. This holistic approach helps users achieve physical and mental fitness.

3. Shifting from Taking to Giving: Julianne recognized that she wanted to contribute and give back rather than solely benefiting from her talents. She shifted her focus from personal success to creating a business that would bring dance and its benefits to the public, helping others realize their dreams and potential.

4. Building a Team: Julianne understood the importance of surrounding herself with a team that could translate her ideas and gifts into a successful business. She sought individuals who complemented her skills and shared her

vision, allowing her to fill the gaps and establish a strong foundation for KINRGY.

5. Scaling Impact: KINRGY initially started as in-person classes but pivoted to an online platform during the COVID-19 pandemic. This shift allowed Julianne and her team to reach a larger audience and impact more lives. By providing dance-driven workouts and fostering emotional connections, KINRGY empowers individuals to believe that anything is possible.

6. Embracing Entrepreneurship: Julianne's journey extends beyond her previous roles as a dancer, singer, and actress. She now identifies as the founder of a thriving business and the leader of a movement. Her entrepreneurial mindset and dedication to her vision have allowed her to create a true next act in her career.

7. Leading a Movement: Through KINRGY, Julianne has expanded her influence and become a leader who helps individuals achieve their dreams and improve their well-being. By leveraging her passion and skills, she has transformed her life and the lives of others, using dance as a universal language of celebration, healing, and connection.

From Reporter to Entrepreneur

1. Identifying Unique Skills: Darren Rovell's ability to recognize undervalued items and tell their compelling stories set him apart. His talent as an information-arbitrage genius allowed him to make profitable investments in memorabilia and build his reputation as a valuable reporter.

2. The Power of Autonomy: Recognizing that Darren's skills could be better utilized in a business context where he had ownership and autonomy, the author encouraged him to make the bold move of leaving ESPN and pursuing his aspirations independently. This decision would allow Darren's mind to roam freely and maximize his talents.

3. Consolidating Achievements: Overcoming the fear and hesitation of leaving a prestigious position, Darren sought to consolidate his gains and leverage his unique abilities to achieve greater success. The desire to take control of his career and make a lasting impact motivated him to pursue new opportunities.

4. Seizing the Perfect Fit: The opportunity to join a young sports gambling company, run its content, and hold an equity stake aligned perfectly with Darren's skills and aspirations. This move allowed him to exercise more control over his business destiny and take ownership of his professional journey.

5. Burning the Boats: By making the leap into entrepreneurship and embracing the risk associated with it, Darren experienced a transformative shift in his life. The decision to leave his comfort zone and fully commit to his own venture opened doors to new opportunities and financial success.

6. Finding Fulfillment and Freedom: Darren's leap into entrepreneurship not only provided financial rewards but also allowed him to pursue what he loves on a daily basis. Taking control of his business destiny empowered him to create a fulfilling career path aligned with his passions and talents.

7. The Best Decision Made: Despite the challenges and uncertainties, Darren considers his decision to take the leap as the best decision he ever made. It brought him satisfaction, personal growth, and the freedom to shape his own professional journey.

Unleashing Your Potential

1. Discovering Uniqueness: Identify what sets you apart from others and recognize your unique position and insights. Determine what you can offer that no one else can, and leverage these qualities to make a significant impact.

2. Embracing Your Specialness: Reflect on your strengths, talents, and passions. Understand what makes you special and how you can maximize those attributes to achieve greatness. Embrace your individuality and use it as a driving force in your journey.

3. Connecting with Inner Desires: Dig deep into your heart and uncover your true desires and aspirations. Reflect on what truly motivates and excites you. By aligning your actions with your genuine passions, you'll find greater fulfillment and purpose.

4. Embracing Uncertainty: Avoid the trap of thinking you have everything figured out. Embrace the unknown and be open to challenges and problems that arise. It is through adversity and uncertainty that your problem-solving skills and ingenuity will shine.

5. Lack of Self-Awareness: Recognize that complete confidence in your plan without questioning it can be a sign of lack of self-awareness. Stay humble, be open to feedback

and new perspectives, and continually reassess your strategies and actions.

6. Problems as Opportunities: View problems as opportunities for growth and innovation. Put yourself in challenging situations that push you to find creative solutions. Embrace the discomfort of not having all the answers and surprise yourself with your problem-solving abilities.

7. Taking Action: Once you have reflected on these questions, take action. Use the insights gained to start burning the boats and embark on your journey. Embrace the unknown, leverage your uniqueness, and pursue your heartfelt aspirations with determination and resilience.

Embracing Insights and Pursuing Boldest Dreams: Stories of Transformation and Growth

1. Rest and Recharge: It's important to take time to rest and recharge, allowing yourself to find joy in the present moment. However, for those wired to constantly strive and pursue new adventures, staying still may not bring the same fulfillment. Recognize the inner desire to continue growing and exploring.

2. Regret and Bold Dreams: The greatest regret people have on their deathbeds is often not pursuing their boldest dreams. Embrace the opportunity to chase your passions and take risks, as it can lead to incredible personal and professional growth.

3. Recognizing Untapped Opportunities: Seize the opportunities that others may have missed. Identify gaps in the market, unmet customer needs, or areas for innovation. These insights can lead to transformative ideas and ventures.

4. Reinventing the Supply Chain: Challenge traditional models and reinvent supply chains to align with ethical and fair practices. By working directly with makers and prioritizing customer values, you can create a differentiated brand that resonates with consumers.

5. Leveraging Social Media: Recognize the power of social media and the importance of

meeting consumers where they already are. Instead of forcing consumers onto owned social media pages, insert brands into conversations customers are having with others. Embrace influencer marketing and leverage the consumer preference for authentic, person-to-person connections.

6. Following Entrepreneurial Paths: Embrace opportunities to build something of your own. Trust your vision and take the leap, even if it means turning down secure job offers. Pursuing your entrepreneurial dreams can lead to tremendous personal and professional growth.

7. Achieving Success and Balance: Balancing personal and professional responsibilities can be challenging, especially as a founder. However, with determination and perseverance, it is possible to build a successful business while maintaining a fulfilling personal life.

8. The Power of Insights and Genius: Surround yourself with individuals who possess incredible insights and domain expertise. Recognize the value they bring to your team and the potential for their contributions to drive success.

9. Embracing Second Chances: Sometimes, individuals have the opportunity to reconnect with someone who previously turned down an offer or opportunity. Appreciate their growth

and success, as they may have found their own
path to greatness.

10. Creating Your Own Success Story: Through
    embracing insights, pursuing bold dreams, and
    taking calculated risks, you have the power to
    create your own success story and make a
    meaningful impact on the world.

Empowering Women in the Startup World

1. Creating a Supportive Environment: Vickie recognized the need to create an environment that allowed her to be the mother she wanted to be while pursuing her career. By starting her own company, she was able to build a flexible work environment that supported both her personal and professional aspirations.

2. Paving the Way for Other Women: Vickie's decision to start an all-female company not only provided her with the flexibility she needed but also served as an opportunity to pave the way for other women in the startup space. She aimed to break down barriers and empower women to balance their personal and professional lives.

3. Overcoming Discouragement: As a female in the startup space, Vickie faced discouragement when it came to starting a family or taking maternity leave. However, she persevered and used these challenges as fuel to create a more inclusive and supportive work environment.

4. Financial Freedom and Success: Vickie's dedication and belief in herself paid off when she sold her company to a major advertising company, WPP. This financial success provided her and her family with financial freedom and opened new doors for her future.

5. Choosing Self-Belief: By choosing to believe in herself and her abilities, Vickie made a life-

changing decision that altered the trajectory of her career. Instead of becoming an employee, she embraced entrepreneurship and unlocked a world of opportunities.

6. Balancing Personal and Professional Life: Vickie's journey highlights the importance of finding a balance between personal and professional priorities. By creating a flexible work environment, she was able to navigate the challenges of motherhood while building a successful business.

7. Inspiring Others: Vickie's story serves as an inspiration to other women in the startup space, demonstrating that it is possible to pursue ambitious career goals while also prioritizing family and personal fulfillment.

8. Impacting the Industry: Through her all-female company and flexible work environment, Vickie has made a positive impact on the startup industry by challenging traditional norms and advocating for gender equality and work-life balance.

9. Encouraging Entrepreneurial Spirit: Vickie's success story encourages aspiring entrepreneurs, especially women, to believe in their abilities and pursue their entrepreneurial dreams. It showcases the potential for personal and professional growth that comes with taking calculated risks and creating one's own path.

10. Achieving Fulfillment: Vickie's journey exemplifies how creating an environment that aligns with personal values and priorities can lead to a fulfilling and successful life, both personally and professionally.

A Journey Driven by Purpose and Empathy

1. The Power of Purpose: Burning the boats is more than just a personal pursuit of excellence; it requires a larger purpose that goes beyond personal enrichment or ego gratification. Having a meaningful goal that aligns with personal values and experiences can be a strong motivating force.

2. Learning from Childhood: Childhood experiences can shape our motivations and drive for making a difference. The author's own childhood, filled with suffering and loss, serves as a driving force to build a platform and create opportunities that can help others avoid similar hardships.

3. No Dream Unfulfilled: Burning the boats is a call to leave no dream unfulfilled and to pursue ambitions without hesitation. It's an invitation to realize the full extent of one's talents and embrace the power to make things happen.

4. Making a Difference: Helping others on their own journeys becomes a higher purpose in life. By intervening and offering support, even through small gestures, one can have a profound impact on the trajectory of someone else's life and provide hope in times of darkness.

5. Healing and Moving Forward: It's essential to recognize that one cannot change the past or

save others from their suffering. Instead, the focus should be on saving those who are currently in need. Finding peace and healing comes from channeling energy towards making a positive difference in the lives of others.

6. Embracing Choices: Each individual has choices to make, whether to intervene or look away when faced with the suffering of others. Choosing to be a ray of light and offering hope can have a transformative effect on someone's life.

7. Finding the Path to Peace: Father Leonir's advice to "go to the river" represents a call to action, to actively engage in helping others and finding one's path to peace and healing. By using personal experiences as a driving force for positive change, individuals can make a significant difference in the world.

8. Never Too Late: It's never too late to start making a difference and pursue a path of purpose. Burning the boats serves as a reminder that there are no limitations on when one can begin their journey to impact others positively.

9. Appreciating Personal Power: Understanding and appreciating one's own power to make things happen is crucial. Recognizing the inherent potential within oneself to create change and positively influence the lives of others is a catalyst for personal growth and fulfillment.

10. Sharing the Light: By embracing the journey of burning the boats, individuals can become a beacon of hope and light for others who are in desperate need, providing support, guidance, and inspiration along the way.

From Central Park to the Vatican: Embracing Global Solidarity

1. The Power of Compassion: The author's involvement with the Global Solidarity Fund reflects their deep empathy for migrants and refugees. Instead of questioning why people are coming, it's crucial to understand the desperation and hardships they are fleeing. The author aims to raise awareness and support for those in need.

2. Transmitting Pope Francis's Vision: As a representative of the Global Solidarity Fund, the author's mission is to convey Pope Francis's vision of equality and global solidarity to a diverse audience, transcending personal religious beliefs. The goal is to inspire others to embrace the message and take action.

3. Going Off Script: During a significant speech in Central Park, the author deviated from the prepared script to connect with the audience on a personal level. By sharing their own experiences of growing up poor and relying on support from a Catholic food pantry, the author aimed to foster empathy and encourage support for those in need.

4. A Private Audience with Pope Francis: The author had the privilege of meeting Pope Francis at the Vatican, where they expressed their gratitude for the support received from their local parish food pantry. The Pope's

humble approach and focus on service to others left a lasting impression on the author.

5. The Power of Solidarity: Pope Francis emphasized the importance of solidarity and intimate engagement with those in need. Bringing the poor closer, both physically and emotionally, is crucial to fostering a sense of connection, hope, and dignity.

6. Remembering the Importance of Human Contact: The author's memories of their mother's longing for human contact, particularly in her final days, highlight the significance of solidarity and compassion. It's not just about financial support but also about offering genuine human connection and care.

7. Embracing the Periphery: Pope Francis's message to go to the periphery resonated deeply with the author. It's a call to extend ourselves beyond our comfort zones, both physically and emotionally, and reach out to those who are marginalized or in need.

8. The Transformative Power of Solidarity: Solidarity has the potential to transform lives, restore hope, and foster a sense of connection. By embracing the principles of compassion and global solidarity, individuals can make a profound impact on the lives of others and create a more just and equitable world.

Embracing Courage: Owning Your Brilliance and Becoming Your Own Platform

1. The Power of Connection: Throughout the book, the author emphasizes the importance of connecting with others. Whether it's the founders and partners they work with or individuals in need of support, forging meaningful connections can lead to transformative experiences and create a positive impact.

2. Meeting Pope Francis: The author had a profound encounter with Pope Francis, who inspired them with his humility, compassion, and emphasis on service to others. This encounter served as a powerful reminder to embrace courage and make a difference in the world.

3. Challenging Risks and Doubts: Leaving the Jets, despite facing criticism and doubts from others, required tremendous courage. The author recognized that their own brilliance and unique abilities were the real platform, not any external entity. Believing in oneself and taking risks is essential for personal growth and success.

4. Embracing Your Brilliance: The author encourages readers to recognize their own brilliance and to take ownership of their talents and skills. By embracing and honing their strengths, individuals can become their

own platform, creating opportunities for growth and impact.

5. Letting Go of the Past: The notion of never looking back is a powerful reminder to focus on the present and future, rather than dwelling on past failures or setbacks. Courageously moving forward without fear of failure allows for personal and professional growth.

6. Being Your Own Platform: Each individual possesses unique qualities, talents, and expertise. By acknowledging and leveraging these strengths, individuals can build their own platform, creating opportunities for success and making a difference in their chosen fields.

7. The Call to Courage: Being courageous is not always easy, but it is necessary for personal and professional growth. By embracing courage, individuals can step out of their comfort zones, overcome obstacles, and pursue their boldest dreams.

8. Empowering Others: Embracing courage not only benefits oneself but also empowers others. By leading with courage and authenticity, individuals can inspire those around them to embrace their own brilliance and pursue their passions.

Final Word

Incorporating key takeaways from successful individuals can significantly enhance our chances of achieving success in life. These principles, derived from various experiences, offer valuable insights that can guide us on our journey towards personal and professional fulfillment.

One important takeaway is the concept of embracing disruption. By recognizing that change is inevitable and adapting to evolving circumstances, we can seize opportunities that arise from disruption. Rather than fearing or resisting change, embracing it allows us to remain agile, innovative, and adaptable in our pursuits.

Collaboration is another crucial element for success. Building strong partnerships and surrounding ourselves with individuals who complement our skills and share our vision can lead to synergistic outcomes. Collaboration fosters collective creativity, problem-solving, and support, enabling us to achieve goals that would be challenging to attain alone.

Pursuing meaningful projects is essential for a fulfilling life. When we align our passions, values, and strengths with the work we undertake, we experience a higher sense of purpose and satisfaction. Meaningful projects provide a sense of fulfillment and allow us to make a positive impact on the world around us.

Moreover, success is not solely determined by external markers such as wealth or status. True success encompasses personal growth, well-being, and a sense of fulfillment. By defining success on our own terms and focusing on holistic well-being, we can lead meaningful and fulfilling lives.

Authenticity and values play a pivotal role in achieving success. Staying true to ourselves, our beliefs, and our values allows us to make choices and decisions that align with our authentic selves. When we prioritize integrity, honesty, and authenticity in our actions and relationships, we build trust, foster genuine connections, and create a positive impact.

Lastly, continuous learning and growth are crucial for long-term success. By embracing a mindset of curiosity, seeking new knowledge, and actively pursuing personal development, we remain adaptable and open to new possibilities. The willingness to learn, unlearn, and relearn enables us to stay ahead in a rapidly changing world.

In conclusion, incorporating these key takeaways into our lives can guide us towards success and fulfillment. Embracing disruption, fostering collaboration, pursuing meaningful projects, prioritizing authenticity and values, and embracing continuous learning are universal principles that can empower us to navigate life's challenges, seize opportunities, and lead purposeful lives. By embracing these principles, we pave the way for a successful and fulfilling journey of personal and professional growth.